Praise for THE DE

An American Tragedy

"Patricia Vaccarino gives us more than a mere account of the events that lead to a brutal destruction of a cultural landmark, a building that was so much more than just a building. Her story is based on her own experience, growing up in Yonkers, and starting her adolescent awakening in the Carnegie Library. Her knowledge is rooted in relationships within the community of real people; residents from various cultural backgrounds. Yonkers was a melting pot of people living together in relative harmony. Prosperity was based on the mutual respect that existed before the special interests moved in—the personal interest of money-grabbing developers in cahoots with the politicians. This group conspired to make money by widening a road which ultimately led to nowhere.

Sacrificing this gorgeous building did not make any sense, and it did not benefit the real community. It benefited a few corrupt individuals at the time, but the damage they did proved to be irreversible. This is very analogous to the era we live today, when community interests are placed on a butcher block in order to benefit a corrupt group of self-serving politicians. Almost like a DejaVu, this type of behavior occurs again and again within our not-so-perfect society."

–Milan Heger, Artist and Architect

"I remember the big oak doors and the windows with the diamond shapes on them. I remember going there for story time. Such a nice place. Warm like a library should be. Being very impressed by the library. It was a lovely place to be. I always felt good in there. One day everybody was talking about it. Suddenly they were talking about a roadway. It was not a satisfactory explanation of what would happen. In my mind, building stuff or creating things, in engineering, there is always a different way, some other way to go. All they really did was demolish an icon in Getty Square a landmark–the library, and they made it sound as if it was monumental and vital to the city."

- **Debbie Bowers Citrone, Educator**

"As a long-time devotee of the Carnegie Library, I devoured **The Death of a Library** eagerly, anxious to learn the true story of why we lost this treasure. Surprisingly, reading this meticulously researched book caused me to experience many of the same emotions I felt as a child climbing the marble stairs to this magical temple of learning, clearly a dominant influence on all our Yonkers lives. Transported to my youth, I was back in the time when imagination and the power of books could take me anywhere.

Vaccarino's analysis of the end of this mystical part of my life was disturbing, bringing back the same feelings of powerlessness I had learning this beloved building was to be destroyed. Filled with nuggets of a powerful, stunning Yonkers history, The Death of a Library opened my eyes to the intricacy of the wide reaching web that caused this betrayal, the devastating destruction of the beautiful landmark of Getty Square, our Yonkers Public Library. The thought-provoking narrative is an essential read for anyone who grew up in Yonkers, lives in Yonkers, or appreciates the intricacies of the rich and complex story that is our Yonkers."

–Mary Hoar, President Emerita **of the Yonkers Historical Society**

"Patricia Vaccarino did a fantastic job in her research and explaining the history of the library right up till the wrecking ball hit it. I did not know the early history of the library, but I was around for its sad demise. I patronized the library regularly for about six months when I was studying to take the police exam. The mention of the movie *GoodBye Columbus* brought back a memory for me. In 1968, after I came back from Viet Nam, I was stationed at Fort Carson in Colorado Springs and I went to see the movie. I was homesick at the time. As I watched the movie there was the Carnegie Library and Nepperhan Ave. Now I'm doubly homesick. Thank you for the opportunity to bring me back to my 'roots' and allow me to enrich my history about the city I grew up in."

–William "Bill" Powers, City of Yonkers Police Officer, retired

"A fascinating and compelling story of how greed, ineptitude, social class and racism let to the destruction of an architecturally and historically significant building in New York State's fourth largest city despite the protests of many of its citizens."
–Michael P. Rebic, former Principal Historic Restoration Planner for the city of Yonkers

"**The Death of a Library:** ***An American Tragedy*** explores the real reasons behind the demolition of the Yonkers Carnegie Library in 1982. The library was a haven for so many Yonkers residents, who were led to believe that the library's demolition was needed in order to widen Nepperhan Avenue and turn it into an arterial. As it turns out, widening the road was only the tip of the iceberg. There were many valiant attempts made by Andrew MacDonald, Michael Rebic, Lee Hipius, Frank Cardone and Henry J. Mazzeo Jr., and others who worked tirelessly to preserve and save the Library. A real departure from Vaccarino's last two fictional works, this is a must read for anyone interested in the political history and climate of 1982 Yonkers and the failed efforts to preserve this magnificent structure, The Carnegie Library."
–-Barbara O'Connell, NYS Licensed Real Estate Salesperson

"A fascinating perspective of how the interests of a few resulted in the destruction of a cherished resource for many. I am reminded of an editorial quote in the New York Times 10.30.1963 'We will probably be judged, not by the monuments we build, but by those we have destroyed.'"
–Angelique Piwinski, a Yonkers Historian

"I was born in Yonkers. The Carnegie Library was one of the most beautifully impressive places I frequented throughout my childhood and early teen years. My peaceful sanctuary. As a preteen, I sat near a window there every Saturday afternoon. It was my naive and innocent goal to read every single book on those massive shelves! After moving thousands of miles away, I heard talk of my library being demolished. This book helps me understand some of the factors and decisions that led to the sadness I felt in losing this piece of history."
–Karen Conroy, Healthcare Professional

"When I was younger, it was my haven. My sanctuary. I can still see the concave marble stairs and wooden bannister leading to the second floor. They are forever 'worn' into my memory. The Yonkers Carnegie Library was that safe, quiet place to go and find a book that would transport me to other worlds…I loved that library."

–Tim Phelps, Former Yonkers resident, Chef-Instructor/Educator

Dear Sarah,
Enjoy The Read!

THE DEATH OF A LIBRARY:
AN AMERICAN TRAGEDY

by Patricia Vaccarino

Modus Operandi Books • New York

 This is a work of non-fiction and the result of many hours of investigative research and witness interviews.

Cover illustration of the Yonkers Carnegie Library and all photos of the Yonkers Carnegie Library are from Wikimedia Commons, the free media repository.

Published 2020 by Modus Operandi Books
www.modusoperandibooks.com

ISBN: 978-0-9963494-9-9
Library of Congress Control Number: 2020925557
Printed in the U.S.

In memory of the Yonkers Carnegie Library

and

For the many Yonkersites who remember what the library brought to their lives

Contents

Introduction

I left my hometown Yonkers at seventeen and never looked back, kind of .... I returned a few times, once to visit my Grandma Katherine, who lived in the heart of the Yonkers ghetto in an old tenement on Jackson Street. Grandma used to shop at a Finast grocery store on South Broadway. I was waiting for her outside of Finast one day when I saw an old friend, Donna Gendelman, carrying an armload of books. I asked her what she was doing with the books. "I'm returning them to the library," she told me. I pointed to the Yonkers City Hall, close to where the library once stood. A hole in the ground was all that remained. I couldn't stop looking at the hole in the ground. I don't think Grandma Katherine could either. Killing that library had hurt her heart. It was one of the few buildings that had been built before she was born in 1909.

No one seemed to know for sure why the library was destroyed. People had been led to believe the library's demolition had to happen to widen Nepperhan Avenue from two to four lanes to create an arterial. The city needed to widen

Nepperhan Avenue to turn it into a major arterial connecting the east side of Yonkers to the west. And this much was true, Yonkers had no direct thoroughfare running east-west. The creation of the Nepperhan Arterial was intended to be a road paved with victory. It meant a return to the good old days when Getty Square was a burgeoning business district inhabited by merchants and shoppers. The new arterial also meant a direct path to the Hudson waterfront that was in dire need for more than just urban renewal. Factories, industrial warehouses and slum dwellings dotting the banks of the Hudson River had been left in a state of deterioration for several decades. The vision for the new Hudson waterfront was grandiose and included a conference center, upscale hotels and restaurants, luxury condominiums, and even a gambling casino. The Hudson River waterfront was designated to become the Yonkers of the Future.

Vision notwithstanding, the true circumstances that led to the death of the library are steeped in half-truths, incredible lies, and wild rumors that range from political corruption to bumbling incompetence. One rumor focused on the true intentions of the Mayor of the time, Angelo Martinelli and his desire to undo the white flight to the east side of Yonkers. Some rumors hinted of racism—and said the people in Getty

Square, called *Ghetto Square* since the late 1970s, didn't need a library anyway. The rumors hinting of racism—the area surrounding the library had become increasingly populated with blacks and Puerto Ricans—could not be easily proven as a reason to destroy the library. Corruption in Yonkers city government had also been alleged, but it's hard to prove people took money under the table, or bribes, without having a smoking gun.

Among the rumor mill, claims persist that Angelo Martinelli wanted to build a bridge from the Yonkers waterfront across the Hudson River to New Jersey, and a sleek high-rise tower to replace both City Hall and the library. Another allegation accuses Yonkers City Council Member Harry Oxman of sacrificing the library to spare his small-time dry cleaning business. And finally, the library itself has been accused of being its own worst enemy.

No one who lived in Yonkers during the library's life can mention its death without getting teary-eyed and choked up. Angry too! Facebook has community groups composed of people who are currently living or had once lived in Yonkers. The largest group, called *I Grew Up in Yonkers*, has over seventeen thousand members. Whenever a comment or photo is posted about the library, there is a flurry of commentary, a collective weeping and gnashing of teeth. Most are unaware of the efforts that people made to save the library. Many years later, crazy speculation about the library's demise still runs rampant. For the record, I made it my mission to find out what really happened. As a kid growing up in Yonkers, the Yonkers Carnegie Library was my first love. The death of this library tugs still at my heart. It is important for you to know that I chose to write this story because if I didn't, then the truth would never have been told.

–Patricia Vaccarino

1
History of the Library: The Face of Democracy

"Every time I see pictures of the library, my heart breaks." - Carol Urban LaConte posted on Facebook I Grew Up in Yonkers April 3, 2019

On a cold day in the Spring of 1982, Mrs. Lee Hipius made her way through the parking lot behind Yonkers City Hall. Small, wiry and compact, the 53-year old Italian-American woman moved briskly in between her mother and her brother, who had joined her on this day to give her their moral support. Lee Hipius's fingers grew numb as she clutched a sheath of papers to her chest. It was not every day that an ordinary citizen gave a presentation at City Hall. While Lee Hipius had always been active in her community, the prospect of talking to a group of public officials made her heart flutter. This April day was mind-numbingly damp with an overcast sky full of grey clotted clouds. Days before it had been unseasonably warm, as hot and as humid as August. The wild fluctuation in temperature was a grim reminder of what T.S. Eliot meant when one of his most famous poems, *the Waste Land*, cited "April as the cruelest month."

Lee Hipius had formed a committee to save the Yonkers Carnegie Library from demolition. As President of the Committee, she had asked the Yonkers City Council if she could make a presentation, but she had been stonewalled. After many months of making polite but persistent entreaties, the City Council finally granted her request. Her tireless effort to save the library was finally paying off. She was so excited to be making a presentation and to be given the chance to save her beloved library. As she came around the corner from City Hall, the moment she saw the library, her excitement quickly plummeted to horror, and she almost crumpled to the ground. Much to her shock, one side of the library had already been bashed in, leaving a mortal wound.

Now ninety, Lee Hipius remembers that April day as surely as it was yesterday. "I did appear before the City Council and talk about how we wanted to save the library. The City Council granted me permission to speak on behalf of the Committee. My brother and my mother came with me. We were approaching it from the Nepperhan Avenue side of the building. When we got up to the library, my mother almost had a heart attack when she saw that the side of the library that faced

Nepperhan Avenue had already been punched out. Until she died, my mother always talked about it—what she saw. They gave us permission to go and plead for the library, but the building had been punched out with a wrecking ball. The message was: 'You can come here and talk all you want but it won't do you a bit of good.' It was a lost cause. It had already all been predetermined."

A few weeks after Lee Hipius made her presentation to the Yonkers City Council, the library was completely destroyed. A grainy black and white photo, taken by the Yonkers Herald Statesman in May 1982, reveals the library's inner sanctum looking as dark as the collapse of a bludgeoned heart. A bulldozer is stuck in the library's entrails. All that remains is a shell-shocked corpse, a pile of rubble, steel girders, twisted coil, shards of granite and yards of broken brick. The petitions and pleas made by the people of Yonkers to save the library had been ignored.

For over a year and a half, Lee Hipius had campaigned to save her beloved library. The Yonkers Carnegie Library, much more than a place to house books, was commonly held to be the most beautiful building in the city. Most other buildings in Yonkers had the look of pedestrian functionality, having served the masses who had come to Yonkers in the early Twentieth Century to work at one of the city's great manufacturing factories: Otis Elevator, The Alexander Smith Carpet Factory and the "Sugar House."

The Carnegie Library building, though, was a sight to behold, a grand object of permanence and beauty, and a beacon of hope in a city that no longer reigned as a queen in manufacturing but was now being savagely torn up in the throes of urban blight and white flight. Southwest Yonkers, where the library stood, had been besieged by fires that only seemed to break out in the middle of the night. Although the fires were caused by arson, no one ever got caught. The fires of Yonkers became legendary. At the time of the library's demise, there were fires everywhere in Southwest Yonkers. Lee Hipius recalls "an awful lot of fires." The frequency of fires prompted the placement of a display advertisement in the local newspaper, the Herald Statesman, to call the local number 423-7100 to report a fire in Yonkers.[1]

As a teen, I remember that in Southwest Yonkers it was not uncommon to see swarms of construction workers, backhoe loaders and asphalt pavers hiccupping tar and smoke, all fueled by demolition fever. The site of a wrecking ball in this part of town no longer looked like a medieval weapon used for mayhem and tribal warfare, but had come to symbolize urban renewal, and the changing complexion of the city from white to

1 Herald Statesman, (hereinafter HS), September 29, 1982, Advertisement.

black and brown. In this city of nearly 200,000 people, racial tensions were as prevalent in 1982 as they had been during the 1960s and 1970s. If anything, the great dividing line between white, black and brown found its epicenter in Getty Square, the heart of the Yonkers ghetto and a five minute walk from the library, and ten minutes from my Grandma Katherine's tenement.

Hardly a crumbling, boarded-up, rat infested tenement, the Yonkers Carnegie Library was in great shape. Color blind, welcoming to all, holding itself above the fray, the library was loved by many Yonkersites, not only Mrs. Lee Hipius. For reasons no one seemed to completely understand, not only did the library now stand in the path of the wrecking ball, but it had already taken a hit without anyone even knowing about it.

In downtown Yonkers, close to the business and shopping district of Getty Square, on the corner of Nepperhan Avenue and South Broadway, the Yonkers Carnegie Library sat next to Yonkers City Hall in the southwestern boundary of Washington Park. Sounds logistically complicated, but it's not. The library had been built in the shape of an octagon to accommodate its small, irregularly-shaped lot. It was no coincidence that the Carnegie Library and Yonkers City Hall seemed to complement one another in the same style of beaux-arts architecture. Both buildings shared the same builder—Edwin A. Quick & Son designed City Hall a few years after the library was opened in 1904. The library, in contrast to City Hall, sat on a hilly bluff that sprawled along the expanse of the corner, as if it was a monument to something much greater than a building. The library's location was said to have lent an 'Acropolis-like' air to the placement of City Hall.[2]

High on the hill, the Yonkers Carnegie Library seemed to see the far corners of the world, beyond the Hudson River, and took Yonkers for what it was—a city hovering in an undefined limbo, blurring the distinction among urban, suburban, and rural; and the rich, middle and working-classes, and ghetto; and the people, black, brown and white. Yonkers had no choice but to relinquish its unique place in this world because it shared its border with one of the largest cities in the world, New York City. Eclipsed by its neighboring cosmopolitan mecca, Yonkers was dismissed as a small city on the river with a funny-sounding name. In spite of the city's inability to achieve prominence in popular culture, the media, or among civic and urban critics, her main public library was undoubtedly grand.

---

[2] The New York Times (hereinafter NYT), April 4, 1982.

I went to the library so often that I can't remember my first visit, but I'm sure it had something to do with Grandma Katherine. I remember its heavy dark wooden doors opening into a hall where Tuckahoe white marble floors mottled with grey veins curved and stretched like a sketch of musical notes. When entering the library's main circulation room, the space felt fully round, but it was actually shaped like an octagon. Small white mosaic tiles were embedded in the floor in large circles and triangles. Stepping into the triangular frames within the circles revealed a decorative border of dark blue mosaic tiles in a classic Greek meander pattern. The library had a familiar scent that was as comforting as stepping into one of the many old public schools that had been built in Yonkers prior to World War II. Many of the city's public schools had been torn down to make way for public housing projects, yet, so far, the library had survived.

The most magical element of the library was the children's room located on the second floor. The children's room had been originally located on the first floor but over time, like most libraries, it had outgrown its space and the children's room was moved to the second floor. The sound of my footsteps to the second floor was hushed by the honed, low-luster, grainy white marble steps. Indiscriminate sharp lines bordered the edge of each step. The vertical-shaped window had frames forming ten panes of a certain X pattern. Sunlight streamed in through the window and fell on the mosaic floor, where the X shapes now seemed to be transformed by the light into the ethereal images of too many crosses to count. As a kid I felt dreamily compelled to count them all while scuffing my feet up the marble steps.

Half-moon-shaped murals, called lunettes, hung from the walls of the children's room. Approximately 26 feet by 4 feet, the lunettes were massive in size, color and imagery. Lunette No. 1 captured Ivanhoe and the Age of Chivalry. I remember the armored knights in battle, tumbling from their horses, and the knight kneeling before a fair lady, and the lore of Native Americans and early settlers on the Hudson River. Lunette No. 2, the Age of Discovery, brought forth the lore of Native Americans and early settlers on the Hudson River. In the Age of Invention that was featured in Lunette No. 3, leading inventors and scientists, most of whom had some sort of historical connection to Yonkers, came together in a hypothetical meeting of the minds.

Every child who grew up in Yonkers during those days remembers the murals in the library. We remember the armored knights in battle, tumbling from their horses, and the knight kneeling before a fair lady. Even many years later, these images are forever burned into their memories as surely as if they were signing up to get a library card for the first time or sitting on the cool marble steps as a way to escape the Yonkers summer heat. There was something about this library that made me feel special, cared for, and as if I was a very important people whose voice counted because I could speak up and ask for a book.

The three lunettes sparking my imagination and the imagination of generations of children like me were painted by artist David C. Hutchison in the 1930s. David Chapel Hutchison was an illustrator, portrait artist and muralist. As a commercial artist, he created covers for several top magazines, including Harpers, Colliers, The Saturday Evening Post and Cosmopolitan. Unemployed like so many during the depression era, he was paid $34 a week through the Works Progress Administration (WPA) to paint the first lunette. Even after federal funds ran out, he completed work on the murals at his own expense.[3]

Luckily enough, David C. Hutchison just so happened to live in Yonkers at 145 Hawthorne Avenue, a five-minute walk to the library. The fact that the artist David Hutchison was originally from Scotland is an amusing detail enhancing the library's lore, especially when another significant

---

[3] **Yonkers Historical Society Newsletter, Summer 1996,** *Carnegie Library Lunettes, p. 3-4.*

connection to Scotland was at the nexus of the very origins of the library. No one could forget that this library was not an ordinary library, but one hatched from the coffers of the wealthy industrialist and Scotsman Andrew Carnegie.

Many accounts about Andrew Carnegie indicate that he was gruff, highly opinionated and acutely aware of his public image to the extent that he was adept at managing his own reputation. The story he told countless times about why he chose to give away millions to build libraries is the grist of urban legend.

Carnegie was the epitome of the self-made man, the classic embodiment of a Horatio Alger rags to riches story. Work hard and you will be rewarded was the canonical lesson he abided by. With hard work, grit and ingenuity a man could accomplish anything. It worked for him and therefore it should work for every man who was intent on bettering his lot in life by embarking on a perpetual self-improvement campaign. As a young boy working in the city of Allegheny, close to Pittsburgh, Pennsylvania, he taught himself with the books he borrowed from Colonel James Anderson, who had opened up his home library to working-class boys.[4]

---

[4] **Jones, Theodore, Carnegie Libraries Across American: A Public Legacy, (New York: John Wiley & Sons, Inc., 1997), 5**

In his own words, "When I was a working-boy in Pittsburg, Colonel Anderson of Allegheny—a name I shall never speak without feelings of devotional gratitude—opened his little library of four hundred books to his boys. Every Saturday afternoon he was in attendance at his house to exchange books. No one but he who had felt it can every know the intense longing with which the arrival of Saturday was awaited, that a new book might be had."[5]

The scant existence of public libraries made it difficult to obtain books. Without Colonel Anderson's generosity, the Carnegie lad would not have had access to a library. Taking Carnegie's thinking to its logical extreme, if it hadn't been for the generosity of Colonel Anderson, the young Carnegie might never have stood a chance to succeed in life.

Later in Carnegie's life when he grew a steel manufacturing company (the precursor to U.S. Steel), his fortune established him as one of the wealthiest men in the world. He tended to be aware enough of public opinion to develop a knack for getting his rags to riches story told and retold in the press. He was also known to freely offer his opinions covering a wide variety of topics: travel, politics, business, economics, labor issues,

---

[5] Koch, Theodore Wesley, A Book of Carnegie Libraries (New York: The H.W Wilson Company, 1917), 8.

international affairs, and getting these opinions placed in speeches, books, magazines and newspapers. In the public eye, he presented a personality in the crosshairs, with two towering contradictions. From one perspective he was the arrogant self-made steel magnate, and from another, he was spare in his words, recounting the working-class anthem of being the self-made man, simple in his gestures and humble to boot.

Communities seeking money from Andrew Carnegie to build a library had to prove they were worthy beneficiaries. Granting the funds to build a Carnegie library meant paying close attention to the community that it would serve to ensure it would represent "a wide range of social and cultural conditions, in their economic base of the communities, in their urban density, in their racial and ethnic diversity, in the age of the community and its cultural institutions, and even in their attitudes towards Carnegie's offer." [6]

From that standpoint, the city of Yonkers was an excellent candidate to get funding from Carnegie. Michael P. Rebic, an expert in Yonkers architecture, wrote about the changing demographics of the city that took place with the influx of immigrants during the latter half of the Nineteenth Century and the early Twentieth

---

[6] **Van Slyck, Abigail A., Free to All: Carnegie Libraries & American Culture 1890 – 1920 (Chicago: University of Chicago Press, 1995), xxv.**

Century. Once home to the gentrified well-born and their sprawling estates, the *City of Gracious Living* metamorphosed into becoming the *Queen City of Manufacturing,* a hub for predominantly Irish, Italian, Jewish, Polish, and Slavic immigrants who came to America seeking jobs and a better life. Due to a critical lack of housing, many families lived in squalor. "In Yonkers, the rapid growth of its population (from 11,484 in 1860 to 79,803 in 1910), the expansion of industry, the almost complete lack of regulations governing building and land use, as well as the overcrowding of workers in tenements, all resulted in the rapid deterioration of the city's urban center during the second half of the nineteenth century." [7]

The overcrowded conditions of workers living in tenements is ultimately what led to the emergence of a public bath movement in Yonkers. Four public bathhouses were built in the Getty Square area to provide a greater quality of life to a population that was ethnically and economically mixed, a true melting pot, the face of democracy, and the perfect sort of community to benefit from having a public library.

The disbursement of funds from Carnegie's sizable fortune was managed by his right arm and

---

[7] **Rebic, Michael P., The Westchester Historian, Quarterly of the Westchester County Historical Society, Volume 62, Fall 1986, Number 4, Yonkers and the Public Bath Movement, 108.**

secretary, the eminently pragmatic and efficient James Bertram. Requirements for the Carnegie library application form were straightforward and simple. "To be eligible, a community had to demonstrate the need for a public library, provide the building site, and promise to support library services and maintenance with tax funds equal to 10 percent of the grant amount annually. Thus, a $10,000 grant required the town to dedicate $1,000 in support each year. If the stipulations were met, the grant was usually approved."[8]

In 1900 Yonkers Mayor Leslie Sutherland, formed a committee with the author and humorist John Kendrick Bangs and the educator Charles E. Gorton, to request funding from Andrew Carnegie for the construction of a library building. The city had to ensure they would pay annual support to maintain and manage the building. In this case, it meant if Carnegie granted $50,000 for the building construction, then the city of Yonkers would allocate $5,000 annually to support the library. Carnegie was often cited as brilliant in getting the benefactors of his grants to assume some of the risk by putting their own skin in the game. Having the community's financial buy-in to pay for management and maintenance delighted Carnegie. It was in complete alignment with his philosophy

---

[8] **Jones, Theodore, Carnegie Libraries Across American: A Public Legacy, (New York: John Wiley & Sons, Inc., 1997), 26.**

of engaging in win-win situations where all of the parties involved shouldered the weight of responsibility. "His one-time grant had to be matched be each community every ten years, an arrangement that the tycoon considered a 'clever stroke of business.'"[9]

Carnegie's grant to the city Yonkers for $50,000 began with a mini-municipal crisis when Carnegie's Secretary James Bertram made a sizable typo in his letter awarding the funds.

A fourth-generation resident of Yonkers, John A. Favareau has worked for the Yonkers Public Library as a reference librarian since 1994. His responsibilities with the Library include custody of the Library's Local History Room. He noted that when author and humorist John Kendrick Bangs had written the initial *ask letter*, he "had asked Mr. Carnegie to extend to Yonkers 'that kind of philanthropic work with which his name was becoming increasingly identified; the letter conveyed Carnegie's offer of $50,000 to provide [Yonkers with] a suitable [library] building.' The only conditions placed upon the gift, as stated in the letter, were that the City should 'furnish a suitable site and agree to maintain a Library at cost of not less than $50,000 a year.' In a related letter from Bangs to the mayor – also presented to the Council – the author and humorist (and former

[9] **Ibid.**

mayoral candidate) pointed out the significant typographical error in Mr. Bertram's letter and assured all concerned that the amount of the building maintenance fund was, in fact, $5,000 and not $50,000."

The error was quickly caught and corrected, but within the context of the life of this library, it was more than a humorous error that was easily rectified; it was another gaffe, one of many to come.

In an announcement made in local press on March 12, 1901, the groundwork for the Yonkers Carnegie library was established. During a Common Council meeting held on March 11, 1901, it was announced that Andrew Carnegie planned to give the city $50,000. *Public Library Building Assured* was the story's headline in the local Yonkers Statesman.[10]

Few other details were released to the press. Most people did not know that the library would soon be moved from a high school building into a new building of its own. Details were kept closely held by the Common Council and Mayor Leslie Sutherland.

---

[10] **Yonkers Statesman, March 12, 1901,** ***Public Library Building Assured.***

Getty Square has always been the hub of the city that reached workers and the gentrified alike. An immigrants' oasis, *the square* as it was called back then, and long before it was called *ghetto square*, connected all parts of the city, north and south, east and west, and it is where many merchants set up shop and small neighborhoods converged into crowded ethnic pockets, heaped one on top of the other. Within two months of the award of the Carnegie funds, the Common Council suggested the library could be placed in Washington Park, and then the expense of seeking an alternate site would be saved. Originally covering about five acres, Washington Park was once the estate of wealthy philanthropist William Fulton Nisbet. The hilly topography of the park did not make it terribly well suited to build a Carnegie library. The press reported that although using this site was certainly cost effective, it was far from ideal. "Such a library ought to be close to and on a level with a street, for the better convenience of the people."[11]

A criterion for the ideal Carnegie library building stated its preference for having its entrance at street level so people passing by could look into the library and be captivated by the sight of many types of people reading books. Unlike other Carnegie libraries, the Yonkers library's

---

[11] **The Yonkers Statesman, Friday, May 3, 1901,** ***Carnegie Library Sites.***

reading room would never be street-level to attract people passing by on the street outside, from the bustling South Broadway. The placement of the library on the odd-shaped lot rimming the outer shelf of a hill in Washington Park was a gaffe. And its crooked lot spilling out to Nepperhan Avenue later put the library at the mercy of corrupt city politics, and in the direct path of the wrecking ball that would eventually take its life.

Not everyone in Yonkers was keen on Andrew Carnegie's largesse in granting the city $50,000 to build a library. Even with Carnegie's carefully controlled public image, there were still many who equated him to be a robber baron who had made his fortune on the backs of the working people.

Across the street from the construction site of the library, Rev. Charley, rector of St. Mary's Church, had plenty to say about Andrew Carnegie. His remarks, recorded in the New York Herald, were made in response to the location of the library which, was directly opposite to St. Mary's Church. "Why is it that so much ostentatious charity and misdirected philanthropy are prevalent in the world today?" he asked. "Does the philanthropist who rears a great library and erects charitable institutions always really love his neighbor in the spirit in which God's law requires? Has the millionaire who blossoms out as a benefactor of his kind toward the close of a lifetime spent in hoarding great wealth, has he, I ask, paid his employees through the medium of whose labor his riches were attained, fair wages to compensate them for their toil or has he remunerated them with a spirit of illiberality? Has his life's path been strewn with acts of simple, kindly charity or has he been grasping and unkind?"[12]

Although Rev. Charley began his tirade by mentioning that he had noticed several women coming hatless to church, his remarks about Andrew Carnegie were as cutting and as scathing as any public chastisement could be in 1902. Despite his detractors, there was no disputing the fact that the wealthy industrialist Andrew Carnegie had risen from his robber baron past like a phoenix from its ashes to become a noble philanthropist. In a seeming turnaround from his earlier days, Carnegie made no secret of his newfound creed that manifested itself in his own statement: "The man who dies thus rich, dies disgraced."[13]

The Carnegie libraries built between 1886 and 1917 have been described "as familiar as old friends." [14] Never ostentatious, threatening or

---

12 New York Herald, Monday, September 15, 1902, Hatless Women from Church, Questions Carnegie Philanthropy.

[13] Jones, Theodore, Carnegie Libraries Across American: A Public Legacy, (New York: John Wiley & Sons, Inc., 1997), 26.

eccentric, the buildings were designed in a variety of classical architectural styles that were intended to be conventional and welcoming. To Carnegie's way of thinking, having libraries in the community was more important than having access to good schools. A child could easily fail in the school system or never graduate but having access to good books was more important than being good in school.[15] Unlike school where a child's temperament had to be suited to the fixed regimen of a curriculum, the library provided the freedom of choice. People could pick and choose what they wanted to learn in libraries and were free to explore their own interests. The library was a temple for people to hone their own unique strengths and talents and empowered them to create their own way of learning, which in Carnegie's estimation was an equal opportunity to all people. Carnegie libraries sprouted up across America and became the true face of democracy.

Although it was Mayor Leslie Sutherland who had helped to initiate building the Carnegie Library, a later Mayor of Yonkers, John Emory Andrus, took credit for moving the library out of a high school and into a new building that was made possible due to the grant from Carnegie.[16]

---

[14] Van Slyck, Abigail A., Free to All: Carnegie Libraries & American Culture 1890 – 1920 (Chicago: University of Chicago Press, 1995), xix

[15] Koch, Theodore Wesley, A Book of Carnegie Libraries (New York: The H.W Wilson Company, 1917).

With little fanfare, the laying of the library's cornerstone took place on Saturday afternoon, June 20, 1903. A copper box filled with various documents was placed under the cornerstone and the public was invited to attend. Local dignitaries included the current Mayor J.M. Walsh and the Chairman of the Library Board John F. Brennan. John Brennan was also known to be a respected attorney and a dedicated civic leader—a true giver to the community. Years later, when he passed away, the courts of the state of New York suspended session the day of his funeral. As could only be expected from a man of Brennan's caliber, the day the library's cornerstone was laid, he dedicated the building to the uplifting of humanity. He said, "All races, the rich and the poor, will be welcomed here."[17]

Officially opening on July 8, 1904, within no time at all, the number of books in circulation increased so quickly that the library was soon running out of space. Miss Helen Blodgett, the quintessential spinster librarian, complained for years that she needed more space to house books, and that something had to be done to remedy the crowded conditions, which she referred to as "growing pains." Right up to the time of her retirement in 1934, Miss Blodgett stayed in close

---

[16] Weigold, Marilyn E., *Yonkers in the Twentieth Century* (Albany: SUNY Press, 2014), 9.

[17] The Yonkers Statesman, June 20, 1903, Carnegie Library.

contact with the local press and reported weekly on the latest acquisitions made by the library as well as its overall increase in both patrons and the number of books in circulation. She also commented on what people were reading and once exclaimed that Yonkersites were reading heavier literature and named Will Durant's *The Story of Philosophy: The Lives and Opinions of the Greater Philosophers* as hugely popular![18]

[18] Yonkers Statesman, January 23, 1929, Library Report Again Decries Lack of Room.

2
Born on the Wrong Side of the Tracks

"I grew up in this beautiful library. I went from the children's rooms to the adult sections over many years and then the stupid city took it away." – Judith Christopher posted on Facebook I grew up in Yonkers May 5, 2015

Fast forward to 1980. Just shy of being eighty years old, the Yonkers Carnegie library held its own, continuing to stand on the hill, housing a trove of books like body armor to protect the city's inhabitants from harm. The message was: All are welcome here. Things did go wrong out there, but the library remained steadfast in its loyal promise to be the one thing in the city everyone could count on. Greater than any one person, the library represented hope, and a window to the future.

More than a splendid beaux-arts style building, the library took on human characteristics, and opened its arms in a graceful hug to all who entered here. A knowing nod, a welcome prayer, a pat on the back, the library was a woman who brought out the best in people because she had hope in all things. A gospel singer who could belt out a spiritual aria taking your breath away, she moved you to a higher level in your own humanity you did not know you had possessed until you heard her song. The library was as wise and as kind as any old woman, black, white or brown, living close to Getty Square. My Grandma Katherine was one of those women. She went to noon mass every day at St. Mary's and always lit a candle for her ten grandchildren, of which I was one, and the unruliest.

In the final years of the library's life, the library's exterior walls greyed with age the same way an old woman bore a few grey streaks in her hair, but she was still beautiful enough to turn heads. Impressive enough to invite the attention of Hollywood, the library's exterior was captured in the film *Goodbye Columbus,* shot there in 1968.[19]

Based on the novel by Phillip Roth, *Goodbye Columbus* spun the yarn of young librarian Neil Klugman, played by Richard Benjamin, who falls in love with a young woman, played by Ali McGraw. Although both are Jewish, the relationship is doomed due to their class differences; he is working-class, and she is from an upscale family in New Jersey. Although this trendy 1960s story focused on a rich man - poor man view of the

[19] **The Herald Statesman (hereafter HS), August 31, 1968.**

world, its central theme related to class and money could easily be applied to the city of Yonkers circa 1982. Only by that time in Yonkers, the real divisions existed among the white east side and everyone else in the west: black, brown, poor white and white working-class. Like Richard Benjamin's character in the film, the library had the misfortune of being born on the wrong side of the tracks.

Even if people in Yonkers hadn't used the library since they were kids, they were aware of its presence as a beacon of hope, sitting on top of the hill next to City Hall. Purely from a numbers standpoint, even though the Getty Square area was considered by city officials to be in sharp decline, the library was still heavily used. Six months before the library was closed, it had 104,425 volumes of books, 704 magazines and 21 newspapers available to patrons. The library was brimming with books and research materials. The reference and technical rooms were usually overcrowded with people. Special programs for children and adults that included lectures, storytelling hours, and movies continued to flourish. The library also provided a much-needed job information center.

Despite its age, the library was beloved by the city's inhabitants and everyone seemed to know it was in great shape. Repairs had been made from time to time, but nothing major. Once the children's room was closed for two weeks while repairs were made to the library's roof. No one could conceive of the library's death. It didn't make sense to tear down such a beautiful building. If my Grandma Katherine knew they were going to take down the building, she never told me. Knowing Grandma's tendency to brood, she thought the library was somewhat like her, the last person left standing in the midst of a war zone.

I don't know if my Grandma Katherine ever ran into Mrs. Lee Hipius, who was determined to save the library from the wrecking ball. As President of the Committee to Save the Public Library, Mrs. Hipius had drafted thousands of leaflets, made countless phone calls and rang doorbells with the tenacity of a politician campaigning for reelection. Only Hipius was no politician. She was a wife, mother of two sons, and part-time office worker. Hipius was not alone in her mission to save the library.

Frank Cardone was born and raised within walking distance of the Library, in the Park Hill "Little Italy" section of Yonkers. As an amateur history buff, (especially of old theaters and Yonkers history), his words are nuanced, and his voice is passionate when he describes the library, "The façade consisted of cream colored brick detailed with local stone: Mile Square granite and fire clay brick from Kittanning, Pennsylvania. Its interior staircases were made from white Tuckahoe marble."

To Frank Cardone the library was more than a beautiful building but the yardstick by which he measured his early life. He spent many hours in this building and in a manner of speaking "grew-up at the library." From the children's room on the second floor (with its three colorful lunettes near the ceiling), to the young adult room and general circulation area, then later as a college student and job seeker after graduation, he spent many hours on the second floor in the business/technical room.

A lifelong resident of Yonkers, Frank Cardone loves his city in all of its historical phases and incarnations. Today he works for the Yonkers Parks Department. He sees the razing of the library to be as devastating as when the movie palace Loew's Theater was torn down in 1974. As a local history buff, he especially loved Loew's Theater, once located a stone's throw from the library, on South Broadway, now gone too, another casualty of the wrecking ball. He says the demolition of this building robbed the city of its finest theater. The building's exterior was decidedly red in distinctive contrast to the lines formed by blue and white bricks. With its high ceilings, balconies and chandeliers and intricate artwork, the grand interior had regal bearing.

Cardone felt that, just like the library, the

theater was intentionally built to be magnificent enough to make every person who walked in feel special for just being there. He lamented that the city lost an excellent opportunity to acquire the theater building and transform it into a cultural center for movies, plays, concerts, large meetings, a mecca for the enrichment of the people in the community. Instead private investors demolished the theater to purportedly revitalize the Getty Square area. A McDonald's and a parking lot took its place on the site where the theater once stood. "You don't know what you have until it's gone," he says wistfully.

He joined Lee Hipius on the Committee to Save the Library because he viewed the library as one of the few architecturally significant buildings in Yonkers. "Along with other Committee members, I spoke before the Mayor and members of the Common Council, urging them to save the building."

Older pictures show a younger Lee Hipius during the time when she was fighting to save the library. For most of her life, her hair has stayed brown and the same length just below her chin. Her eyes are as wide and as expressive as her smile. Her Roman nose and olive-toned skin attests to her Italian heritage, although she admits there might be a little bit of French Canadian blood coursing through her veins. All of her life she has been a doer, a woman who did everything, managing the house, the kids. She was a den mother for her sons who were boy scouts and had made countless contributions to the Catholic Church. Her dining room had lace curtains, an extra layer of plastic on the lampshades, and photos framed in old tarnished brass. A hutch cabinet is full of gold-rimmed fine china that she probably used on holidays and holy days of obligation. Her home shows the full visceral impact of a Yonkers Italian-American household in the Twentieth Century. She looks fiercely determined, full of pride, the right person to take on City Hall to save the library. Her library. Everyone's library.

The Saint Patrick's Day Parade in March 1982 had given Lee Hipius and Frank Cardone the opportunity to walk among the people on the street to get them to sign their petition. This was pre-internet, when a grass roots campaign could only be done by being out in the public and catching the ear of anyone who would listen. The St. Patrick's Day parade in Yonkers was a big deal back then. Everyone seemed to march in it or showed up just to watch the spectacle. It was the perfect venue to churn public opinion and lobby for a cause. Hipius remembers darting in between the rows of the Ancient Order of Hibernian bagpipes, Catholic school girls wearing crisp white shirts under woolen uniforms and white gloves, and the Yonkers Pops Marching Band blaring Broadway show tunes, and out of the crowd and speaking to people about the library, gathering as many signatures as she could. There was a collective denial about the impending destruction of the library. No one believed it would really be torn down.

3
Knocked Flat to the Ground

***I went to School 10 right up the street from it. So, I was no stranger to the Carnegie Library. I remember asking my mom why was they knocking down our library when I seen the construction crews out there in 82. And I remember thinking to myself when I went to its new location. "They tore down that beautiful structure, for this?? this??..😌😒"*– Gilbert Soto posted on Facebook I Grew Up in Yonkers February 28, 2018**

It's odd so many people did not believe the library would be demolished when its doors had officially closed. The year before it was destroyed, the Yonkers Carnegie Library closed on May 2, 1981. Its contents were removed and placed in a new makeshift downtown branch. Called the Getty Square Branch on 7 Main Street, the new site had once been a department store, first Genung's and later Howland's. Both stores had gone out of business. The move to this new temporary library meant more room for books, activities and library staff.

But before the new library branch on Main Street opened, Lee Hipius recalls a fire breaking out. "The contents of the Yonkers Carnegie Library were stored at a department store in Getty Square that had gone out of business. The books and card catalog cabinets were put inside of the in the empty building. It was a temporary set-up. I did actually go there. I can't recall how long it was before the fire. There was a fire of some kind. I believe the fire broke out because there were index cards in the drawers. Too bad; even those drawers were lost because of the fire."

The empty shell of the department store needed renovation to open as the new branch library for the Getty Square area. The city then spent approximately $500,000 to buy the Howland building after the store went out of business, and another $500,000 was spent on the building's refurbishing. The project was carried out by the Community Development Agency (CDA) and paid for with federal funds.[20]

The reference to federal funding reveals a strong clue as to why demolition fever was running rampant in Southwest Yonkers. It's always important to keep in mind that construction of the Nepperhan arterial was being done by the City of Yonkers in conjunction with New York State under the guise of urban renewal. The Community Development Agency (CDA) was involved with

---

[20] **HS OCT 28, 1979 Library Relocation Project in Full Swing by staff writer Jim Cavanaugh, Library Relocation Project in Full Swing**

this library renovation and often involved whenever the city accepted federal funding to build another low-income, public housing project in Southwest Yonkers. From this standpoint, any urban renewal project was a money maker for the city of Yonkers and New York State.

Crushing accounts of the doomed Carnegie library had been extensively reported in the press. Two years before the library was demolished, Herald Statesman staff writer Jim Cavanaugh wrote in glowing terms about the prospect of the Carnegie Library being "knocked flat to make way for a new arterial road." Cavanaugh suggested Andrew Carnegie would have approved of the demolition, and wrote, "A self-made steel millionaire, Carnegie appreciated the progress—the kind of progress the Nepperhan Arterial can apparently bring to downtown Yonkers."[21]

Although Cavanaugh was a reporter, he added commentary suggesting that he was biased in favor of the grand vision for the new Hudson River waterfront that seemed to be slated as the Yonkers of the future. He suggested Carnegie would have enjoyed knowing that the tons of books being moved into a department store had a connection to steel. "Besides, he'd have the satisfaction of knowing that once the tons of books are moved to their new home in the former

---

[21] **Ibid.**

Howland department store in Getty Square, they will still rest on the Carnegie name—literally."[22]

Cavanaugh's sentiment was echoed by Joseph Pagano, the city's program manager in charge of the library project. "Look at these girders. I haven't seen them like that since they [put] up the last subway," [he] remarked, pointing to the words 'Carnegie USA' emblazoned on the metal frame of the former department store.[23]

The disastrous outcome of the building's remodel turned the earlier exuberance expressed by Cavanaugh and Pagano into foolish prattle. The extensive remodeling that had been done for $500,000 [or more] left poorly applied plaster and water stains on walls. Paint peeled off in sheaths. Open holes in the floors exposed electrical cables and industrial debris. Two old boilers in the flooring below the basement were not operational. One could be repaired but the other could not. But the most embarrassing gaffe turned out to be when the floors of the old department store could not support the weight of all of the books moved from the Carnegie library to this new site.[24]

Frank Cardone recounted, "Because of a strict limit on how much weight stress the floors in the building can handle, book stacks had to be

---

[22] **Ibid.**
[23] **Ibid.**
[24] **HS Oct 26, 1980 Shoddy work Mars Library Renovations.**

limited to five shelves. Consequently, the new library's book capacity was no greater than that of the old. The irony is that one of the reasons for a new library was to provide additional space for books." As it turns out, later accounts reported that the Getty Square Branch held far fewer books than the old Carnegie library.

The department store still had an escalator running through its core that went to the upper floors. Without windows or natural light, the children's room now sat in the basement where its only exposure stared into a sewer pipe. The good news was that the water pumps in the basement were made operational so they could pump out the flooding that occurred during heavy rainfalls. Even after renovation was completed, many rooms had evidence of water leakage and cracks in the walls. The Getty Square branch was intended to be temporary and only last for a few years but ended up staying in the Genung's building for twenty-one years.[25]

Even at the eleventh hour as the Yonkers Carnegie Library lay on death row, Editor and General Manager of the Herald Statesman David I. Hartley wrote about the history of the library, describing it as a landmark. "The old Yonkers Public Library is a landmark, everyone agrees. But

---

[25] Ibid.

it's a landmark caught up in the kind of progress that tramples the past in the name of the future."[26]

Having landmark status was one more critical detail that went missing in action. The Yonkers Carnegie Library was never legally declared to be a landmark. Another gaffe? Or was it intentional that the city never applied to have the library accorded landmark status? Marilyn E. Weigold, who wrote *Yonkers in the Twentieth Century* and is also a professor at Pace University, recounted the testimony of former employee of the library Rhoda Breitbart. Ms. Breitbart's take was they didn't have enough time to really seek national historic register status. "That everything happened quickly. They're just wasn't enough time."[27]

Some suggest it was intentional that the library had not applied for landmark status. Andrew MacDonald, who was a Yonkers City Council Member during the time period when the Yonkers Carnegie Library was demolished, said, "The city didn't want to apply for landmark status because knew they were going to take the building down."

The City's plans for the Yonkers of the Future were revealed in the press as far back as 1965 [when] "the city had reportedly set its sights

---

[26] **HS, April 18, 1982, Worthy Goal, dim outlook.**

[27] **Interview with Marilyn Weigold, July 5, 2019**

on a 21-million arterial highway program that awaited funds from New York State to widen Nepperhan Avenue."[28]

On April 26, 1966, the city's Director of Planning, Philip R. Pistone, revealed an ambitious master plan to build an arterial loop around Getty Square that would divert traffic from that congested area. Phil Pistone called for the state arterial to go west on Nepperhan Avenue, pass City Hall and proceed through the site of where the Public Library stood.[29]

Yonkers Librarian John Favareau noted how the idea of the arterial was floated as early as the mid-1950s but wound up for some time on the back burner. Then things started to pick up in the early 1960s during the era of urban renewal. Money problems seemed to have delayed the actual construction of the arterial until the early 1980s. In addition to slicing the heart of the library in two, the city knew as early as October of 1966 that 300 families would be displaced to clear the way for the route of the arterial. In examining two maps that planned the expansion, the Yonkers planning department clearly charted the route. Phil Pistone was the head of the Yonkers planning department. Under his direction the route cut right through the library.

---

[28] **HS Westchester Commerce & Industry, January 19, 1965.**

[29] **Herald Statesman, Yonkers, N.Y., Tuesday, April 26, 1966, Community Renewal Program Offers Hope for Downtown**

Throughout America, and historically, the public library has always been integral to the community and considered to be a force for good. "In school buildings, for instance, the library was often located in a room that functioned primarily as a classroom, limiting library use to after-school hours."[30] City halls and country courthouses offered social libraries the double advantage of official government sanction and rent-free accommodations but were often accompanied by their own brand of inconvenience. In Hamburg, Iowa, for instance, the library was forced to share its small space, which was also used for a ladies' resting room and for various meetings. Just as often, libraries were forced to confront the more noxious aspects of town life. In Hamilton, Montana, the library was "housed in a small room" behind the city fire department in the city hall, adjoining the same room "where the horses are kept," while in Macomb, Illinois, the library was on the same floor with the city council rooms and city prison.[31]

Unlike other Carnegie Libraries that performed double-duty by providing a shelter for imminent civic needs, The Yonkers Library served no purpose other than being an outlet to circulate books. Even though Phil Pistone's plan meant

---

[30] Van Slyck, Abigail A., Free to All: Carnegie Libraries & American Culture 1890 – 1920 (Chicago: University of Chicago Press, 1995), p. 130.
[31] Ibid.

demolishing the library, he suggested that this was an essential ingredient of good downtown planning. Pistone readily admitted that his own plan extended the downtown Nepperhan Avenue Arterial that had already been planned by New York State.[32] No consideration was given to what the library meant to the people of the city of Yonkers. Through the years, the library had come to represent a vision for the future that incidentally was grounded in the past. But other people had a much different vision of what the future should be, and it meant obliterating the past.

Despite reports made in the press, most people were largely unaware that New York State bought the building in 1971. When the state took title to the building, the city was paid $335,000. Three years later, the state charged the city $1,100 monthly rent for keeping the library there.[33]

Once the library building was ceded to New York State, there were no other indications that the death of the library was imminent. In the 1970s, the city had spent $600,00 to prepare plans for building a new library. At one point, more than $400,00 had been spent to retain the celebrated architect I.M. Pei to design plans for a grand civic center-library complex, but nothing materialized, purportedly because the city had run into financial

32 The Herald Statesman, April 26, 1966, Community Renewal Program Offers Hope for Downtown.

33 HS, April 18, 1982, Worthy Goal, dim outlook.

problems. Being beset with financial problems was *de rigueur* for the city throughout the 1970s and 1980s. A later project to build a new library along with an 18-story county office building was spearheaded by the Community Development Agency. This time Yonkers architect Joseph Roth was paid $200,000 to design library plans. The city had hoped to get federal funding under the Public Works Program, but again nothing materialized.[34]

Frank Cardone has no recollection of a Committee to Save the Library forming in 1971. Certainly, he would be aware of such an organization. "I would not be surprised if everyone at the time thought that it would be many years before anything came of the plan and that the library would be safe," he said. "I also believe that human nature is such that many people must have felt there was no way they will demolish that beautiful building. Someone will see the light and insist that the state change its plans for that intersection."

It was taken for granted that this urban renewal project, called the Nepperhan Arterial, was critical to develop more industry and commerce on the waterfront.[35]On the surface, the creation of the arterial seemed to be the only way to drive east –

---

34 HS Oct 26, 1980 Saga of Yonkers library: Continually On the Move
35 HS Westchester Commerce & Industry, January 19, 1965.

west without hitting the muddled quirks peculiar to Yonkers geography.

4
Nothing is Level in the City of Hills

"Yonkers politicians at work [in] the city of hills where nothing [is] on the level ."- Steven Keindl posted on Facebook I grew up in Yonkers May 5, 2015

Yonkers is an old American city that harkens back to the colonial era. My Grandma Katherine didn't drive, so she walked everywhere or took the bus. Downtown Yonkers in Getty Square was somewhat akin to Greenwich Village because of its narrow streets and alleys and many pre-war buildings. The Getty Square area was a hodgepodge of stores, tenements, and old apartment buildings, a cornucopia of small merchants and retailers. What made Yonkers exceptional and different from many other cities was its many hills. Mary Hoar, President Emerita of the Yonkers Historical Society, told me that the city "built the streets on cow paths and Native American trails."

Unlike the large sprawling cities of Los Angeles and Denver, Yonkers is small and compact, measuring only about three miles wide, five miles long, taking up a total area of approximately eighteen square miles. The northwest and southwest portions of the city are flanked by the Hudson River, and on the east by the Bronx River. The Saw Mill River is the natural dividing line between east and west Yonkers. Further divided by natural ridges and valleys, Yonkers is congested with many small rolling hills. At the mercy of an unforgiving geography, neighborhoods are tranches, and tend to evolve as stubborn silos that are worlds apart from one another, culturally and economically.

With its narrow streets, hairpin turns and one-way streets going nowhere, it has always been hard to get around Yonkers. And still is today. The city's inhabitants back then often spoke pridefully for having so many impossibly steep hills. Like Rome Italy, some called Yonkers the city of seven hills: Nodine Hill, Park Hill, Church Hill, Cross Hill, Glen Hill, Ridge Hill and Locust Hill. A popular urban legend claimed Elisha Graves Otis chose Yonkers to build the first elevator because he had been inspired by the city's many treacherous hills.

While traveling from the east-west has always been fraught with bottlenecks, the streamlined north-south thoroughfares such as the Bronx River Parkway, the New York State

Thruway, and the Sprain Brook Parkway, along with excellent passenger train and bus service, has always given people easy access to New York City.

From the mid-1960s until around the time of the library's demise, there was no apparent plan to develop an effective mass transit system beyond buses. There was certainly no initiative to resurrect the Yonkers Trolley system, which when you think about it, made all the sense in the world to chug up and down the city's many hills with the same historical panache and efficiency as San Francisco's streetcars.

Instead of developing an effective mass transit system, the city's inhabitants were at the mercy of inadequate roads to handle the increasing load of traffic. So, it was completely logical for the city to seek funding from New York State to build a road that was streamlined for efficient travel east - west, even if that meant sacrificing the library. And as far back as anyone can remember, New York State Governor Nelson Rockefeller was chagrined by the circuitous, snake-like travel it took his limousine to go from the east side to the west side of Yonkers. Some say, anecdotally speaking, that the notion to create a Nepperhan arterial, albeit a state route, came from the top.[36]

This urban renewal project, called the

[36] Interview John Favareau Local Historian, Yonkers Public Library June 3, 2019

Nepperhan Arterial, never got off the ground, but no one seemed to ask why, and more importantly, the library lived on. Suddenly, in the 1970s the old plans conceived to widen Nepperhan Avenue to create the arterial resurfaced. But because it had been talked about for years, no one believed it would really happen. According to former Yonkers City Council member Andrew MacDonald, "I was a young corporate lawyer and on the City Council part-time. It was my first time on the Council. The arterial coming up Nepperhan was going to be widened to the river, from two lanes to four lanes. I was opposed to it, but I couldn't get any other support. Got help from the Yonkers Historical Society. The state had money to widen the arterial. The issue was where it was going to go."

By April 1982, the clock was ticking down on the library. Lee Hipius and Frank Cardone, along with other members of the Committee had gathered over 5,000 signatures for the petition to save the library. I like to think Grandma Katherine ran into Lee Hipius at the parade and signed her petition. It really didn't matter how many people signed the petition, it would never be enough to stop the City from cleaving the library's heart in two. The City, New York State, the real estate developers, Mayor Angelo Martinelli and the majority of the Yonkers City Council didn't care about what the library meant to the community.

Mayor Angelo Martinelli and the majority of the Yonkers City Council envisioned an arterial that would cut a swath through the site of where the library stood. Officials with New York State also had a stake in wanting to see the library go down. The state had a vested interest in collecting federal funding to get the arterial built. Collectively, the politicians, bureaucrats, real estate developers, contractors and construction teams had a grand vision for the city's nearly 200,000 inhabitants. And no one knows for sure if money, or how much money, changed hands in order to get the deal done.

"The library was beautiful inside and out," Andrew MacDonald said. In the final weeks, he tried to save the library. MacDonald and another council member, Charles Cola, brought forth a resolution to try to rescue the library from demolition. Andrew MacDonald (Democrat) was elected in 1979 and began his term, representing the 3rd Ward in 1980. Charles Cola (Republican) was 6th Ward councilman in 1982. Their bipartisan resolution was intended to stop the destruction of the library. Given the state's ownership of the building, its demolition had been accepted as a fait accompli, and there had not been a required vote to agree to the demolition. "At this point, the library's contents had already been relocated to the old Genung's (Howland's) building," Andrew MacDonald said. "So, by bringing a resolution, there was one more chance to stop the demolition."

"Demolition began the following month making clear the decision was already made and nothing could stop it," Frank Cardone said. "I suspect that we were unaware of how far the process had reached. Our committee was formed at the eleventh hour and fought the good fight, but it was simply far too late."

5
Make Downtown Yonkers White Again

"I thought it was a castle. I loved it there." – Karen Hrizo Marchewka posted on Facebook I grew up in Yonkers, February 17, 2018

Andrew MacDonald's attempt to save the library didn't mark the beginning of a beautiful relationship with Mayor Angelo Martinelli. In January 1982, Martinelli had begun his new term as Mayor. He had previously been Mayor from 1974 to 1979, sitting out 1980-81 after losing the 1979 election to Gerard "Gerry" Loehr. While Loehr served as a one-term mayor from 1980 to 1981, Angelo Martinelli labored noisily and confrontationally to reclaim his former post. It was during this time that the plans that had been percolating behind the scenes for the Yonkers waterfront began to emerge. Angelo Martinelli's second phase as Mayor lasted from 1982 to 1987, long enough to see the demolition of the library and the creation of the Nepperhan arterial, a state road that ultimately would lead to nowhere.

Short, stocky and barrel-chested, Angelo Martinelli was known to speak loudly with the rapid delivery of an automatic weapon. Brash and opinionated, his operating style bore the signature of an early Trumpian leader, although he never cast his eye to be anything other than the Mayor of Yonkers; there had been a brief attempt to run for Congress, but for the most part city politics seemed to be the height of his ambition. The way Martinelli managed the city won him many enemies and just as many friends. His opponents call him a "demagogue who was full of hot air," a way of saying he was full of bluster and a bullshitter. His fans claimed he was "a folksy and robust leader."[37]

Before he became Mayor, Martinelli was a media mogul and a printer. Often describing himself as a millionaire businessman, Martinelli owned his own publishing and printing firm, Gazette Press, that printed everything from magazines, flyers, business cards and letterheads. Shortly after winning a comeback reelection in 1981, Martinelli bragged that he beat his opponent, one-term Mayor Gerry Loehr, because he could print so many more campaign flyers, post cards and door hangers. In his own words, Martinelli considered himself to be "too forceful and

[37] **HS Nov 16, 1981 Angelo R. Martinelli** ***Mayor-elect talks candidly about himself.***

domineering." He stated, "That might be good in business, but it's not a good way to lead a city."[38]

He owned three magazines: *Stock Market Magazine*, *Westchester Illustrated*, and *Hudson Valley Magazine*. From his years of working in the media, he knew how to position himself to the public and the press. He was known to be fond of a wall hanging on his office door that read: "If you're being run out of town, get in front of the crowd and make it look like a parade.[39]

Regardless of his persona and operating style, Angelo Martinelli was big on progress. It's probably not a coincidence that the old 1960s plans conceived to widen Nepperhan Avenue to create the arterial resurfaced when he was Mayor during his first phase from 1974 to 1979. His vision for the future borrowed heavily from the legendary urban kingpin Robert Moses, who had a well-practiced pattern of putting up high-rise buildings and building mega superhighways. Moses also had a penchant for isolating people of color in public housing projects. The superhighways Moses built were intended for the car-owning white middle-class.

In the case of Yonkers, the state arterial allowed for safe passage from the east white side to southwest Yonkers, without ever having to

---

[38] Ibid.

[39] Ibid.

navigate the side streets where low-income public housing projects were mostly inhabited by people of color, young families and old-timers like my Grandma Katherine. By 1963, more than 80% of the city's existing or planned public housing was located within a several-block area of Southwest Yonkers,[40] which was walking distance to the Carnegie Library.

Throughout the 1970s, the city continued to concentrate its public housing development in Southwest Yonkers. Packing all of the poor into one area of the city set the expectation that only people with low incomes were welcome here. Setting a rigid low-income standard stifled the opportunity for people to achieve upward mobility. A sign could have read: *You can only rent here if you're poor and black.* Anyone else didn't fit in and felt forced to move out. There was no incentive to buy a home in the neighborhood. Many single-family residential homes had been replaced by high-rise public housing projects. The inventory for homes was extremely limited, and when homes were available, people of color were often restricted from getting financing due to redlining practices. The low-income public housing projects did not have front stoops or back stoops, greenbelts, gardens or community areas—this discouraged people from developing a sense of community.

---

[40] **Yonkers 1996. US. V. City of Yonkers 96 F.3d 600, (2d Cir. 1996).**

Public housing projects were a disaster that caused private prejudice, white flight, real estate steering, bank redlining, income differences, and self-segregation.[41] Instead of becoming communities where people could grow and flourish, Southwest Yonkers turned into a stew of crime, delinquency and despair.

With due credit to Angelo Martinelli, he strongly advocated during his campaign that the city needed to impose its own moratorium on subsidized housing. When he took office as Mayor in January of 1974, no additional projects were approved for a number of years.[42]

Under Martinelli's leadership, the proposed Yonkers waterfront plan was intended to leapfrog over the ghetto-ridden Southwest Yonkers, including Getty Square. The provisions set forth in the Yonkers Waterfront Plan that allowed business, entertainment and retail to flourish would whisk well-to-do white residents from the east side over to the Yonkers of the future, thereby bypassing the spoils of segregation. When subsidized housing development for families resumed in the late 1970s and early 1980s, during a time when Martinelli was still at the helm of city government, Yonkers continued to confine its development of subsidized housing to Southwest

---

[41] **Rothstein, Richard. The Color of Law, (New York: Liveright Publishing, 2017), vii, viii.**

[42] **Yonkers 1996. US. V. City of Yonkers 96 F.3d 600, (2d Cir. 1996)**

Yonkers. Staunchly refusing to erect public housing on the predominantly white east side, the city was eventually embroiled in a high-profile lawsuit brought by the U.S. Justice Department that dragged on for years and was ultimately not settled until 2007.[43]

During the years when Angelo Martinelli was Mayor, only a few people can attest to what went on behind the scenes that resulted in the death of the library. Aside from Lee Hipius, Frank Cardone and Andrew MacDonald, there was one other high-profile person who had tried to save the library. Michael P. Rebic worked for the city of Yonkers for about ten years as the Principal Historic Restoration Planner. Rebic is also the author of *Landmarks Lost & Found: An Introduction to the Architecture and History of Yonkers*, and several scholarly historical articles about Yonkers, the working-class and the public bath house movement. During the time period when the Yonkers Carnegie Library was demolished, Rebic reported directly to city planner Phil Pistone.

Rebic was often privy to many of the planning decisions examining the best way to revitalize the downtown area. And yet despite his proximity to the locus of power in the planning department, Rebic was not privy to everything. The city government of the time had departments

---

[43] **Ibid.**

that functioned in silos kept as far apart as some of the neighborhood tranches in Yonkers. From a planning perspective, people only knew about things going on in their own silos and did not necessarily know what was really going on in the big picture. For example, Michael Rebic was not aware that the library was no longer owned by the city but had been sold to New York State in 1971.[44]

Press photos of Pistone show a man whose face was dominated by a large nose that looked as though it had been broken more than once. Yonkersites would describe Pistone as looking like his face had been punched in by a bag of nickels. Despite his gruff appearance, Pistone was kind to Michael Rebic and donned a paternal air; he counseled Rebic that if he only came up with one good idea a month, that was good enough. Rebic describes Phil Pistone as "one of the best bosses I've ever had." But unknown to Rebic, it was his boss who had drawn the plans to destroy the library.

Building a road through the site of the public library? No one took these plans seriously. Even Rebic said, "He [Phil Pistone] had never mentioned to me that he was a proponent of the plan to extend the arterial into the middle of Getty Square." Ironically, it was Pistone who had hired Rebic as an Historic Restoration Planner. It was

[44] **Interview Michael P. Rebic June 1, 2019**

inevitable that, sooner or later, Rebic would have to deal with the prospect of razing the library, the exact type of historic building he had been hired to save.

Rebic describes himself back in 1982 as a "young and callow lad." Not a native of Yonkers, but a resident of the Upper East Side of Manhattan, Rebic commuted each day to work for a city that was in the throes of a chaotic transition. "The city neglected the entire western side," Rebic said. "People were made to believe the downtown area was dangerous and there was 'political leadership' that led people to believe that by demolishing buildings and making the area more suburban, then the area would thrive. One Yonkers Mayor [Angelo Martinelli] said that we needed to put a monorail around downtown Yonkers, which was a complete joke in the planning department for the city where I worked. I remember saying 'that this sounds like George Jetson's future of Yonkers.'"

The Yonkers of the Future was admittedly part of the focused agenda for Angelo Martinelli. Martinelli did not create the slumification of Southwest Yonkers; instead he had inherited the problem. Dismayed by the droves of white flight from downtown to the east side of Yonkers, Martinelli aimed to revitalize the Getty Square area to make it great again. He had a vision for Yonkers that was sleek, ultra-modern, and would bring the city into a new age of prosperity, a return to the glory days when Yonkers was called *the city of gracious living.*

Anyone who knew Martinelli spoke of his driving desire to increase the city's tax base. Increasing the tax base would result from new job creation, increasing the number of gainfully employed people, and attracting new business to the city's downtown area, and especially to the waterfront where industry had languished. Real estate development was of paramount importance, not only to increase the city's revenue stream, but also to lay the groundwork for the city's future. Out with the old, in with the new.

For a long time, rumors persisted that Angelo Martinelli wanted to build a bridge to New Jersey, but that wasn't true. It was also said that Martinelli dreamed of replacing the City Hall building, which was as antiquated as its nearby companion, the Carnegie Library, with a towering skyscraper constructed of chrome and glass, but this was originally the vision of another Yonkers Mayor, John E. Flynn (1961-66), who was affectionately known as "Chippy." What Martinelli really wanted was to make Yonkers great again, which was code for make downtown Yonkers white again.

6
Yonkers of the Future: Jane Jacobs vs. Robert Moses

"I grew up in this beautiful library. I went from the children's rooms to the adult sections over many years and then the stupid city took it away." – Judith Christopher posted on Facebook I grew up in Yonkers May 5, 2015

Part of Michael Rebic's job as Principal Historic Restoration Planner was to preserve as many historical buildings as possible. Like Lee Hipius, Frank Cardone and others, he recounts that the juxtaposition of the library and city hall located together up on a hill, "sat like the acropolis of Yonkers." He said, "Some foolish politicians thought simply expanding the roads to downtown Yonkers, which was an extremely vital place but not by 'white' American middle-class standards; that is, there were "ethnic shops, etc.—all of which would be considered an asset now—but the difference was class and racially based—downtown was extremely vital—just with the 'wrong people;' they thought that if they brought more cars and people down, and if we had that monorail, everything in downtown Yonkers would be wonderful."

The city planners didn't take into consideration what would be good for the community. As a city that had always hovered among urban, suburban, and rural; and the rich, middle and working-classes and poor; and the people, black, brown and white, the new plan further isolated Southwest Yonkers; its public housing projects, slum dwellings, and some buildings that were rundown but could have been renovated. "The idea was to "suburbanize downtown Yonkers; to make it acceptable to people who, I believe, had fled their previous neighborhoods because of bad, governmental decisions as to what an 'area' should look like," Rebic said.

The development of the Yonkers waterfront appeared to be a stunning revitalization of the city, but beneath the surface, it denied the needs of the growing population in Getty Square in order to create a new suburb, a white enclave, separate and unto itself, on the river. Little attention was paid to meet the needs of the Southwest Yonkers community because the race to the Yonkers of the Future was on.

The controversy surrounding the Yonkers of the Future was highly symbolic of the opposing philosophies of two remarkable people: Jane Jacobs and Robert Moses. Jacobs has been described as a powerful activist and community organizer who took on city hall and won. Self-taught, Jacobs was a brilliant observer of what made cities work, and flourish. Her books and articles are held to be legendary among urban planners, architects, designers, academics and civic leaders. Moses, the autocratic city-planner who bulldozed homes and buildings, destroying neighborhoods, had amassed enormous dictatorial power over the urban development of New York City from the 1930s to the 1960s. At one point, he concurrently held a dozen high level administrative positions that gave him the money and the power to create New York City according to his own whims and vision.

Mayor Martinelli saw the Yonkers of the Future very much the same way Robert Moses would have viewed the city, as slash the old, build modern roads and buildings, and contain the ghetto. Jane Jacobs, on the other hand, advocated for "mixed uses" so that different types of people would be drawn to a place like Getty Square at different times of day and night, and for many reasons, such as business, entertainment, shopping and dining-out. She also opted for an area to have a healthy mixture of old and new buildings, so one enhances the other, and to promote an entrepreneurial mindset and environment by including ample low-rent space for small businesses and startups.

Jane Jacobs often noted that short, intimate blocks were an ingredient in a healthy urban neighborhood. Long arterial types of streets are not inviting to, nor safe for pedestrians. After Nepperhan Avenue was widened, pedestrians were not made welcome to cross the new arterial, nor could they safely cross the street. "The widening of Nepperhan Avenue was a real big question," Rebic said. "I remember sitting in meetings with that—the avenue can only be so wide. We've tested this and some old woman needs to be able to go from one side to the other in time to make the traffic light. At my age [back then], I couldn't make it across the street in time before the light changed." After Nepperhan was widened, my Grandma Katherine could no longer cross that street. She was always afraid of getting hit by a car.

The Jane Jacobs idea of a healthy neighborhood teems with vigorous street life. Jacobs' neighborhood of the old Greenwich Village had a quaint similarity to the old Getty Square with its narrow winding streets full of local shops and small eateries; multiple generations and old-timers living there seemingly forever; and people from all walks of life, economically, ethnically, racially, rubbing shoulders with one another. Knowing one's neighbors, looking out for one another, and developing a sense of community is what happens organically in a vital city when people are interacting with one another on the street, and not when people are their cars, driving from one suburban bubble to another.

Jacobs often favored libraries as essential to a community. Even if libraries were no longer in operation and had been re-purposed for some other civic activity, the library's presence served as a strong reminder of the power of its legacy and what it stood for—free to all, a face of democracy. In a city already fragmented into silos due to its geographical composition of tranches, enclaves, valleys and hills, the razing of the library created one more dead zone in Southwest Yonkers. Jacobs would not have been a fan of Yonkers Planning Director Phil Pistone's master plan for Yonkers that he revealed to the press in 1966. Nor would she have been enamored by Angelo Martinelli's vision for Yonkers of the Future and would have viewed it as a homogenous theme park for middle-class white people.

In Rebic's estimation, "The Carnegie Library came down because the city believed that larger roads would bring more commerce and revitalize the old downtown. They were hoping more businesses would move into the area, and also hoping that maybe they could remove all of the minorities that they had in the past. They already received federal funds to build housing for these minority groups that were largely black and Puerto Rican."

Robert Moses once said, "Majorities, of course, start with minorities." He could have been talking about Yonkers. Minorities are never too threatening when they are really a minority. Their assimilation into the existing culture is often novel and can even be exciting, but once a minority starts hitting its stride, becoming more visible and prominent, then fear and loathing permeates the preexisting culture because the status quo of the majority, in this case the white majority, was being threatened.

How skin color played into this library saga would be impossible to examine without looking at the numbers. The U.S. Census reports of 1960 and 1980 attest to the increase dramatic increase of minorities in Yonkers. So does testimony filed in the lawsuit (U.S. V. City of Yonkers 96 F.3d 600) brought by the U.S. Department of Justice against the city for racial discrimination in housing and education. "The period between 1960 and 1980 was marked by striking demographic shifts in the city as a whole, and in the Southwest in particular. During those years, and particularly beginning in the mid to late 1960's, the citywide minority population increased by 325%, and 94% of that increase was concentrated in Southwest Yonkers. During those same years, Southwest Yonkers also lost nearly half of its white population, resulting in a total rise in the level of minority concentration from 6.7% to 40.4%. The population of East and Northwest Yonkers, in contrast, remained overwhelmingly white."[45]

---

[45] **Yonkers 1996. U.S. V. City of Yonkers 96 F.3d 600, (2d Cir. 1996).**

7
Racism: The People Didn't Deserve a Library

"I loved that library." – Dennis Dudley posted on Facebook I grew up in Yonkers May 5, 2015

Was racism a factor in the death of this library? The idea that racism played a role in the death of this library has been asserted as true, yet it has also been sharply refuted. Former City Councilman Andrew MacDonald doesn't think so. During his bid to save the library, the issue of race never came up. Yonkers Public Librarian and Local Historian John Favareau indicates the plans to demolish the library had been developed in the mid-1960s and before the rush to get federal funding for the rash of low-income public housing projects that sprang up in Southwest Yonkers during the wake of demolition fever. Comments have been made on the Yonkers community page on Facebook that the people down there (meaning people of color in the Getty Square area) didn't deserve a library.

Frank Cardone, the Yonkers history buff

who played an active role in trying to save the library, said, "I see no relationship between the demolition of the Carnegie Library and the dramatically changing demographics of downtown/Southwest Yonkers. The Carnegie was replaced by the one in the former Genung's department store on Main Street. This new location opened in 1981. Both buildings were convenient for anyone wanting to use library resources in west Yonkers." Cardone also noted that patrons using the new library on Main Street had an easier time finding parking there.

Jeffrey Williams grew up in Runyon Heights, a small enclave that was the only black community located in the predominantly white east side of Yonkers. Williams went to Yonkers schools, graduated from Saunders high school, a trade school, where he first became interested in architecture. Later he studied architecture at Pratt Institute in Brooklyn and spent six months studying architecture in Rome. When he came home, he found himself interested in what was happening in Yonkers and went to work for the Community Development Agency (CDA). He wound up staying with the city of Yonkers for 12 years, working for Planning Director Phil Pistone as an urban designer, and working with others, including Michael Rebic. "I was always intrigued with where the library was placed," Williams said.

"That place intrigued me. The building interested me. That was my local library. I wound up spending extra time there. I spent afternoons after school, a couple hours every day, then get on the bus and go home."

Later Williams was a senior urban designer, and eventually staffed the city's landmark preservation board. Once Michael Rebic had left his post with the city, Williams assumed Rebic's position. Many years after the razing of the library, Williams served as the Commissioner of Planning and Development for the city of Yonkers. Williams also served as the first black president of the Yonkers Historical Society in 2008.

When Williams was asked if it was possible that the library was demolished due to racial motivations, i.e., Getty Square had turned into a ghetto, he was circumspect, indicating there was "no racial connection, not for that particular project."

There were, however, some overtones when discussion focused on rebuilding the library. The site in the old department store on Main Street was intended to be an interim gap until a new permanent library was built downtown. Behind the scenes, discussion in the planning department hinted that the local residents wouldn't take advantage of the library. According to Williams, "There were off-handed comments. They didn't say the community didn't deserve it. I don't think it was something said in a formal meeting I participated in. It was more like offhanded comments. It's fuzzy as to who said it."

Tony Clark also grew up in the Runyon Heights enclave of Yonkers. Today he is an attorney and owner of the Chicago-based Clark Legal Group, a law firm that specializes in family law. "I grew up in Runyon Heights that was predominately black. I thought we all decided to live there. I didn't know it was intentionally segregated."

Clark has encyclopedic knowledge of how racism factors into Yonkers' history and notes how in Homefield and Lockwood on the east side of Yonkers, there were restrictive covenants that said you could not sell to a black person. This restriction was in place and tethered to the property because they didn't want to get a bunch of people from Harlem. "It was odd," Clark said. "They never took them [the restrictive covenants] away. It was on their deeds and after the civil rights act in 1964 they couldn't enforce them. Until I went to law school and became a lawyer, I learned some of the legalities that went on in that part of Yonkers."

Clark also knew Winston Ross, the head of the Yonkers NAACP who played an integral role in bringing the lawsuit against the city for public housing discrimination and in education.[46] Clark said, "Wilbur Ross lived around the corner from me and his brother tried to date my sister!"

Just for the record, Clark makes it clear that contrary to one Yonkers urban myth, Al Sharpton did not file the lawsuit against the city. "Some people in Yonkers had it that Al Sharpton filed the lawsuit, but this is erroneous."

Another historically significant case involves the plight of Joshua Cockburn, who was a black man put on trial for violating a common deed covenant attached to all Edgemont Hills properties that forbid Negroes from owning or renting there. Edgemont Hills is a suburban development located on the Scarsdale/Greenburgh town lines in Westchester County, New York. The case took place in the 1930s when Pauline Cockburn purchased property located on the border of Scarsdale and attempted to build a home with her husband Joshua. A neighbor complained that the presence of Negroes was in violation of the deed covenants that restricted people of color from living there unless they were employed as servants. Ultimately, Pauline and Joshua Cockburn prevailed in the courts and were allowed to stay at their home, but not without undergoing a messy legal fight that dragged on for years.[47]

---

[46] **Lohud, Sept 8, 2015, Yonkers Civil Rights Activist Winston Ross dies.**

The plight of the Cockburns in 1936 might seem preposterous within the context of the Twenty-first Century; the case certainly predates the razing of the Yonkers Carnegie Library in 1982 and can be relegated as an embarrassing story that can be stowed away in the annals of Westchester County history. Except racism can never be brushed aside as historical ignorance, especially not when it has never been eradicated in America and continues to rear its ugly head. In fact, one outrageous episode of racism took place in Yonkers in 1979, the same year final plans were being made to shut the Carnegie Library. Greater than an isolated act of racism, this hate crime led to a bizarre sequence of events that revealed just how deeply racism had been ingrained in the Yonkers culture.

While people of color were tolerated in the small pocket of Runyon Heights, they were not tolerated in the rest of east Yonkers. Racism had long been part of the social fabric of Yonkers and was often cited as the chief reason why low-income, public housing projects never got off the ground on the east side of the city. City Council members, who represented predominantly white wards in the east, made certain that public housing projects stayed west, particularly in Southwest

---

[47] **The Secret History of Scarsdale, August 13, 2014, Joshua Cockburn The Final Voyage as Captain of the Yarmouth and the fall of Marcus Garvey.**

Yonkers. Black, brown, and white were segregated by the natural boundary of the Saw Mill River Parkway. Racism impacted more than the development of low-income public housing. It turned out to be deadly too.

One hot, sticky August night in 1979, an arsonist torched the home of a black family. Thomas Porter, an executive at IBM, had purchased a home in the predominantly white enclave of Colonial Heights in East Yonkers. After a long day of moving into their new home, the Porter family woke at four in the morning to find their home engulfed in flames. Mrs. Porter was hospitalized with severe burns on her face and arms. The Porters' two children and a niece and a nephew also suffered burns. Their new home was completely destroyed.[48]

At first it was reported that the home had been firebombed, but later accounts indicated the house had been doused with gasoline. The city's response to the Porter fire was to issue a public statement. An open letter advertorial was published in the Herald Statesman and signed by the usual litany of current city, county and state politicians, including Mayor Angelo Martinelli, deploring the outrageous act. Later Martinelli was instrumental in expanding the $25,000 reward, initially offered by IBM, to anyone who had any

---

[48] **HS August 13, 1979 Firebombing!**

information in connection to the crime.[49]

The Yonkers Police immediately suggested that the crime might not be racially motivated and was intended to target the previous owner who had sold the home to the Porter family. The suggestion was farfetched, especially given that the original owners had to have moved out of the home after the real estate transaction closed. Typically, there is a wait period between the time the sellers move out and the buyers, the new owners, move in. It just isn't plausible for the arsonists to have been targeting anyone other than the Porter family.

The day after the fire, the Yonkers police apprehended three young men who happened to be riding around the neighborhood with burglary tools and five one-gallon cans of gasoline. After being questioned, one at a time, the trio had an iron clad alibi; they were siphoning gas. The police determined "their story was too good to be concocted." Detective William Kennedy of the police-fire arson squad said, "We interviewed each one, and they each told us the exact same story. I buy their story."[50]

The suspects had a receipt from an all-night Pathmark supermarket to show they were purchasing cold cuts and rolls when the fire erupted. Further investigation indicated that

---

[49] **Ibid.**

[50] **HS August 9, 1979 3 eliminated as suspects in fire which drove out family**

Pathmark employees corroborated their story. Presumably, the three boys carrying gas cans and burglary tools in their car were at the Pathmark all night buying cold cuts and rolls. Besides, police suspected that the true arsonist(s) made their getaway in a stolen red Thunderbird that was found five blocks away and later spotted by witnesses, because it too had been torched, only causing about $500 worth of damage. It was concluded that the two fires were related.[51]

To date, the arsonist who torched the Porter home was never found. "There were lots of fires around the city at that time," Lee Hipius had recalled. Some fires might have been accidental, but it was no accident that killed 87-year-old Mary Altero Riccardi on July 25, 1979. Her home was torched and destroyed on purpose. Waves of suspicious fires were linked to the Nepperhan Valley Arsonist who, to date, was also never found. Mrs. Riccardi lived at 608 Nepperhan Avenue in Southwest Yonkers which was in the heart of the burgeoning ghetto. In Yonkers there were always rumors afoot that fires were deliberately set to pave the way for the groundbreaking of yet another low-income housing project, but in the case of Mrs. Riccardi, today the site of her former home now belongs to the city of Yonkers and is occupied by the Yonkers Organic Yard, a

[51] Ibid.

composting and recycling station, and an adjacent dump.

Mrs. Riccardi's grandson, Richard Riccardi, blasted politicians, especially Mayor Martinelli, for not making a big enough deal about his grandmother's death. He felt that the political outrage expressed for the black Porter family was conspicuously omitted for the old white woman. Riccardi emphasized his grandmother had actually died in a fire, unlike the burns suffered by Mrs. Porter, causing him and his family immeasurable grief, but the politicians had short-shrifted her because she was not black.[52]

Never mind that the arsonist who torched her house didn't target her because she was white. There is a greater likelihood that the arsonist targeted Mrs. Riccardi's house because she lived in a predominantly black neighborhood. During this time period, there was a pervasive feeling among many Yonkersites, especially among the white working-class, that people of color got all of the breaks—free housing, free schooling, free money (welfare, health care and food stamps), i.e., a free ride. The white working-class credo further asserted that they had to work for everything to achieve a come-up, while people of color were lazy, good-for-nothings perpetually seeking handouts.

---

[52] **HS August 17, 1979 politicians again assailed in arson death aftermath**

While it's ridiculous and irrational to suggest that blacks got all of the breaks even when it came to how black and white victims of arson were reported in the press, this racist mindset further emboldened the deep racial divide, not only between the east and west side of Yonkers, but one that still exists today throughout America, and has always been on the brink of tearing the nation apart.

Racism impacted more than the development of low-income public housing and heinous individual acts of racism; it led to racial segregation in the public school system. It wasn't until the landmark case, United States v. Yonkers Board of Education, brought by the Justice Department in 1980 that the city's long-standing practice and pattern of racism was identified and proven. The city's decision to place low-income public housing only in Southwest Yonkers was so pervasive that of course it led organically to the to racial segregation in the city's public schools.[53] After all, these were the days before mandatory busing, and children tend to go to schools in the neighborhoods where they live.

When people of color who lived in Southwest Yonkers were herded out of their older tenements and into public housing projects, the outcome was the creation of a ghetto. In her body

---

[53] **United States vs. Yonkers Bd. of Educ. 624 F.Supp. 1276 (1985).**

of work, Jane Jacobs often noted how low-income projects become "the worse centers of delinquency, vandalism and general social hopelessness than the slums they were supposed to replace."[54]

Originally when Michael Rebic was hired as a consultant by the city, his salary was paid through a federal program. The federal government realized they were beginning to destroy downtown Yonkers. Rebic said, "They hired people like me to assess which buildings should be saved. I remember telling one employee: 'I said no you can't sign these things off and postdate them. I need to see them before I sign off on something. You just can't tear something down.'"

Rebic remembers going into some of those houses in the Getty Square area and Warburton Avenue to decide if they were architecturally important or not. He had been led to believe that the homes had been reduced to squalor and expected filthy conditions, but they were extremely clean. "They might have been small, etc., but I was shocked at the cleanliness," he said.

My Grandma Katherine's tenement was so rundown that her old boiler blew up and she had no heat. She lived alone on the ground floor. The house was too much for her, but it was the only

---

[54] **Jacobs, Jane, The Death and Life of Great American Cities, (New York: Random House, 1961),6.**

home she knew, and she did her best to keep it clean. Most of her neighbors, who were black, looked out for her. Dogs ran wild on Herriot Street. One day a dog bit her and took a chunk of flesh out of her leg. One of her neighbors took her to the emergency room to get her stitched up.

In Yonkers circa 1980-81 racism was more often subtle than it was blatant and out in the open like the Porter fire. It's not as though heinous acts of overt racism were commonplace. Unlike the south and other parts of America, as a city in the north, Yonkers had never enacted Jim Crow laws. The Yonkers Carnegie Library never had a "Negro" reading room like the segregated libraries in Gainesville, Texas or in Santa Fe, New Mexico. Some libraries created separate library services for black patrons. The Gainesville library's Negro reading room never was used to segregate black patrons. Instead, in 1924, library service for black readers was established in the Negro school house.[55]

Downtown Yonkers, Getty Square, did have all of the elements of a genuine community, of which the library stood at its apex between north and south, and east and west. Greater than any one person, faith, or organization, the library was the active center for the community because it was free and open to all.

55 **Van Slyck, Abigail A., Free to All: Carnegie Libraries & American Culture 1890 – 1920 (Chicago: University of Chicago Press, 1995), 158.**

But according to Michael Rebic, although the community was thriving and business was thriving, the people were not the right color. "The Getty Square area was especially hard hit and eventually, all of western Yonkers was completely neglected by the local politicians, and especially by Angelo Martinelli, who at that time was Mayor. Eastern Yonkers hated western Yonkers, which had been at one time one of the richest areas. Of course, it was racially motivated. Western Yonkers was largely becoming black and Puerto Rican and there was tremendous discrimination. This type of discrimination went on in every American city; the discrimination in real estate in Yonkers is really a metaphor for America."

Former Yonkersite Sidat Balgobin recounts that his mom used to work in the library, and how it was a shame to tear down such a beautiful, historic building. "Yes, widening for the road," he remembered. Over fifty years later, he still remembered the library and going upstairs to the children's room. Although Sidat Balgobin grew up in Yonkers, he eventually moved to Norwich, Connecticut. His mother, Pearl Balgobin, worked at the circulation desk of the Yonkers Carnegie Library for about ten years.

Both of Sidat Balgobin's parents were from Trinidad. He grew up across from Trevor Park on Warburton Avenue in the 3rd Ward section of

Yonkers represented by Andrew MacDonald. Close to the Getty Square area, Warburton Avenue ran parallel to the Hudson River and was in the zone slated to become the Yonkers of the Future.

Balgobin recalls living amid a mix of Catholic and Protestant families, and all types of ethnic backgrounds. "For me, it was kind of a 'Leave it to Beaver' kind of thing," he said. "As children, my friends were just my friends. I was blissfully unware of the prejudice. I didn't grow up with the experience of prejudice. The only incident I personally recall is when our landlords rented an apartment to our family. It turned out the reason they rented to us was because they didn't like their neighbors."

Pearl Balgobin loved going to work every day. Balgobin said his mother couldn't believe she was getting paid to do this work. "Working for the Yonkers Carnegie Library was a wonderful environment and a beautiful building. The only reason why she left her job was to move to Florida. Somehow, we knew the library was slated for demolition. Had my mother stayed in Yonkers, she would have tried to save it."

Sidat Balgobin's recollection of the library is one more story expressing astonishment and sadness over the loss. There is a collective disbelief among Balgobin and others who grew up in Yonkers that such a thing could have happened.

Urban renewal destroyed so many of the beautiful homes on Palisade avenue. "These homes were torn down to make way for six-family apartment buildings where they crammed people into small spaces. At one time, the whole area was beautiful," he said.

When asked how the library ended up becoming demolished, Balgobin declared, "I don't know what happened behind the scenes. Follow the money. Who profited from the library being torn down? The demolition of the library might be related to housing discrimination."

Yonkers Carnegie Library on the corner of Nepperhan Avenue and South Broadway (1978)

Main Floor and Circulation Desk Facing Northeast (1978)

Interior Staircase Leading to the Second Floor (Children's Room) (1978)

Second Floor, Children's Room (1978)

Side Entrance Facing Nepperhan Avenue (1978)

APPARENTLY A LOST CAUSE — Petitions and pleas of the public aside, this bulldozer was on the job Monday to begin the demolition of the former Yonkers main library building on South Broadway. The project is to clear the way for the Nepperhan Arterial.

Demolition of the Yonkers Public Library, April, 1982 (Photo from the Yonkers Herald Statesman)

8
Democracy vs. Capitalism

"Martinelli was Mayor and this was one of the many crimes that could only happen in Yonkers. That building was historical and had no business of being demolished." - Stephen Treacy posted on Facebook I grew up in Yonkers April 29, 2019

The death of this library is a metaphor for the age-old struggle in America between democracy and capitalism. "There was a conflict between a very vital downtown area in western Yonkers and the middle class residents and political power base of eastern Yonkers," said Michael Rebic. On one hand, there were the many faces of Yonkers, black, brown and white, who revered the library and benefited from all it had to offer. On the flip side, there was big money to be made. The federal government and New York State would be funding the demolition of the library and the road construction. Developers would make money and construction crews, still unionized, would get paid. By taking down the library, everyone got a cut.

Michael Rebic noted, "The reality is urban renewal was nothing but transferring land from poor ethnic communities to investors. It's America at its best," he said, sarcastically. "Look at what happened to New York City— [Urban Renewal] wiped out ethnic communities and people made money off it!"

While Martinelli was mayor in 1979, a group called Yonkers Waterfront Associates was given the exclusive rights to develop the waterfront. The award to Yonkers Waterfront Associates was made without public bidding, sort of a wink, a nod and a handshake done behind closed doors. Yonkers Waterfront Associates was given the exclusive rights for 90 days to determine whether the 60 acres of waterfront could be developed to accommodate a $45 million luxury hotel, conference enter and retail center.[56]

In September 1979, the month after the Porter fire and around the same time that the Genung's/Howland department store was being renovated to be the new site of the downtown library, the waterfront project began to take shape and form. Plans were unveiled showing more than a conference center, a riverfront hotel and space for retail outlets. Now a restaurant was added to the specs. It would take an estimated $45 million to complete the project. Costs would be split 50-50 between Yonkers Waterfront Associates and the city of Yonkers. The city intended to get a significant portion of its share through state and

---

56 HS May 25, 1979 Developers eye site on waterfront—given exclusive rights!!!

federal urban development grants. The projected cost did not include the land acquired through condemnation proceedings.[57]

Much of the groundwork for the Nepperhan arterial and the proposed waterfront project had already been laid before Angelo Martinelli lost his bid for reelection in 1979 to Gerard Loehr, a reserved Yonkers attorney who came from a family with roots in municipal government. His grandfather, Joseph F. Loehr, was Mayor of Yonkers during the 1930's and, before that, city comptroller. His great-great grandfather was a member of the city's Common Council.[58]

During Loehr's one term as Mayor, from 1980-81, he suffered blistering attacks from Martinelli that are reminiscent of Trumpian rage. Loehr countered Martinelli's attacks by accusing him of cronyism and corruption. During the time while Martinelli was not Mayor, acting City Manager Eugene Fox signed a deal giving Yonkers Waterfront Associates exclusive rights to develop a $160 million project on the waterfront.[59]The original deal that proposed a $45 million project had now escalated to be a $160 million. At the same time that the waterfront deal was inked, the disastrous renovation work done on the new library in the Genung's building had delayed its

---

57 HS, Sept 12, 1979 $45 million proposal unveiled for waterfront
58 NYT, April 17, 1981, Harassed Mayor Rolls with the Punches
59 HS, Sept 23, 1980, Developers Ink Agreement on Proposed Waterfront Center

opening, causing the old Carnegie library's lights to stay on, but it's reprieve from death row was only temporary.

Although Martinelli didn't formally sign the waterfront deal, it was undoubtedly his handiwork. Yonkers Waterfront Associates was Martinelli's top pick among real estate developers. As soon as Angelo Martinelli got his post back and took office as Mayor in January 1982, the old 1960s plans conceived by Phil Pistone and others to widen Nepperhan Avenue into an arterial resurfaced with swift vengeance. Since the real estate deal had already been done, it was full speed ahead.

In retrospect, one reason why Martinelli ruthlessly campaigned to unseat Loehr is because he stood in the way of Martinelli's deal making to develop the Yonkers waterfront. As a lame duck Mayor, Loehr had tried to terminate the city's contract with Martinelli's preferred developers, Yonkers Waterfront Associates. "Yonkers' ambitious $163 million waterfront project is not feasible and the city's contract with private developers should be mutually terminated," Loehr said in a carefully worded statement after he lost reelection to Martinelli.[60] Once again, the proposed price of the project changed to $163 million.

It just so happens that the principal of Yonkers Waterfront Associates was Melvin

---

[60] **HS, Nov 17, 1981, Loehr Proposes Scrapping Waterfront Proposal**

Weintraub, a close personal friend and business associate of Angelo Martinelli. The friendship between the Mayor of Yonkers, Angelo Martinelli, and real estate developer Melvin Weintraub spanned for decades and lasted until both men were in their nineties. Both men were born in the Bronx and had a lot in common. To borrow a quote from the power broker Robert Moses, "It is safe to say that almost no city needs to tolerate slums. There are plenty of ways of getting rid of them."[61]

Martinelli's vision for his Yonkers of the Future was to create a suburb on the river that would be built around the slum or rather in spite of it. Melvin Weintraub made money off of slums. He had a penchant for identifying and buying slum dwellings in need of rehabilitation. He was also highly adept at getting loans from federal and municipal urban renewal programs to fix up these buildings. His idea of renovation was often the equivalent of plastering scenic posters over the slum dwellings so from a distance the boarded up, burned-out tenements would look like a row of town houses with white clapboard shutters and small pots of flowers in the windows. In other words, he took out loans for buildings, but often didn't do anything to fix them, and when the time came to pay back the loans, he didn't. Nor did he

[61] **The Atlantic, January 1945, Slums and City Planning by Robert Moses**

pay taxes on these buildings. It wouldn't be fair to call him a con man, and suggest he was making money on the backs of the white, black and brown, poor and working-class. As a real estate developer, Weintraub was a cunning dealmaker who knew how to talk big and make a quick buck from government money.

Due west of the greenbelt of Washington Park, where the Yonkers City Hall and the Carnegie library sat together like an old married couple, Martinelli fervently believed the Waterfront project would rescue Yonkers from its chronic budget shortfalls and never-ending financial crises that had plagued the city during the entire time he had reigned as Mayor. Martinelli's vision was laudable; the waterfront was a stunning concept and it was a viable solution that would bring money and jobs to the city. Except the numbers, size and scope of the project kept changing and Melvin Weintraub's dubious track record made him the worst possible choice among real estate developers.

In fact, it was a tad odd for Martinelli to align himself with Weintraub because Martinelli enjoyed architecture that was visually stunning and luxurious. As the principal of the Morelite Construction, Weintraub was little more than a slum lord. His buildings, the ones he actually renovated, were, at best, mediocre in design, stark-looking, low-cost public housing projects. Martinelli did not seem to be put-off by Weintraub's lack of experience with luxury real estate. Nor was Martinelli put off by Weintraub's track record of developing real estate projects that were only funded within the purview of government-issued loans and grants. Even Weintraub's tendency to be litigious never posed a red flag to Martinelli. Whenever Weintraub didn't get what he wanted, he immediately threatened to sue. Weintraub ascribed to the *threaten them, sue them and make them pay* philosophy of business——the same operating style practiced by Roy Cohn and Donald Trump. But the most potent foreshadowing of the doomed relationship between Melvin Weintraub and the city of Yonkers stemmed from Weintraub's past indictments alleging fraud.

As early as 1972, it was reported in the New York Times that Melvin Weintraub and his brother Gerard Weintraub were among eight indicted in New York City loan scandals. "They were the largest borrowers from the $135-million Municipal Loan Program, which was set up to provide long-term, low-cost loans to owners of slum buildings unable to obtain money to rehabilitate their buildings through ordinary commercial channels. The Weintraub brothers obtained 21 loans totaling $15,100,500. Additional charges included alleged mortgage frauds, grand larceny, offering false instruments for filing, misrepresenting architects' fees and of giving unlawful gratuities to a city employee."[62]

It soon came to light that Melvin Weintraub was involved in another complication tarnishing his track record as a real estate developer. Doing business as Morelite Construction, Weintraub was the developer of several federal building rehabilitation projects and embroiled in a dispute with New York City over payment of $6 million in loans and taxes that the city says is owed but Weintraub says is not. Weintraub's defense against the city of New York soon came to sound like the battle cry of Fake News! He continued to shower the press with entreaties, portraying himself as a model developer.[63]

If the public, the press or the city administration and Council doubted Weintraub's ability to implement Martinelli's vision for the waterfront, misgivings could be put aside the moment Weintraub formed powerful strategic alliances. He lent credibility to his posturing as an upscale real estate developer by taking on two respectable partners, Henry Silverman and Peter Edelman, who were principals of S-E Asset Management of Manhattan. Both had previous

---

[62] **NYT, Jan 19, 1972 8 Indicted by City in Loan Scandals**
[63] **HS Oct 17, 1979 Waterfront Public Hearing**

experience with larger-scale projects, particularly with developing retail complexes. The new entity formed by Morelite Construction and S-E Asset Management is what became the new legal entity, Yonkers Waterfront Associates.

New partner in the venture Peter Edelman protected the viability of the project by being vague about Weintraub's involvement. Edelman said the city will share an, as yet, undecided share of the profits and said he did not know what role Morelite Construction would play in the actual building of the project.[64]

Months later when Weintraub was asked about allegations that he owed nearly $4 million in unpaid real estate taxes to New York City, he said, "Those newspaper articles are totally untrue. They are politically motivated by politicians in New York City. Let me assure you Morelite or Mel Weintraub has never defaulted on any project in this country." Weintraub maintained that "the whole mess will eventually be settled in court," and "that he would be the victor."[65]

Then Henry Silverman, one of the new principals, who was brought into Yonkers Waterfront Associates to lend credibility to the project was found to have been the subject of several investigations in New York City. The

---

[64] Ibid.
[65] HS Dec 4, 1979 CDA Inquiry

Yonkers Herald Statesman reported: "Silverman's company, the Convenience and Safety Corporation, had won an exclusive franchise under very questionable circumstances by the Board of Estimate to furnish 4,100 bus shelters in the five boroughs. It was charged that Silverman's company was awarded the franchise due to influence peddling with several prominent city and state political figures.[66]

Soon both new venture partners Peter Edelman and Henry Silverman would leave Yonkers Waterfront Associates in a cloud of mounting scrutiny and controversy. At this point, things should have started to fall apart in the deal between Yonkers Waterfront Associates and the city, but it didn't. It's essential to keep in mind that the award made to Yonkers Waterfront Associates had been made without going through a public bidding process. Since it was widely known that Martinelli and Weintraub were good friends, the deal smacked of cronyism, but no one was shouting, at least not yet. Melvin Weintraub was still officially in charge of making Angelo Martinelli's waterfront dream come true.

In later commentary, Martinelli was defensive about being named as the signing party who inked the deal. He was quick to point out that he was the first official to discuss the development

[66] HS Jan 21, 1980 Waterfront Questions

proposal with Yonkers Waterfront Associates and was the catalyst but stressed it was former City Manager Pat Ravo who entered into the 1979 agreement on behalf of the city, giving Yonkers Waterfront Associates the exclusive development rights.[67] And it is worth mentioning that in less than a year City Manager Pat Ravo would leave his job under a cloud of scandal for misappropriation of funds amounting to millions of dollars.

Other press accounts indicate it was acting city manager Eugene Fox who had signed the first contract with Yonkers Waterfront Associates. Whether it was Eugene Fox or Pat Ravo is inconsequential, because it was always clear that the deal was done at the behest of Angelo Martinelli.

Every agreement between the city of Yonkers and Yonkers Waterfront Associates specified that the deal was exclusive for a limited time period, usually ninety days. By April 1980, it had taken nearly a year for Yonkers Waterfront Associates to deliver a marketability study. Weintraub's group continued to receive 90-day extensions to complete a study and to seek financing. And over the course of six years, from 1979 to 1985, every time an announcement about the project was reported, the numbers related to how much it would cost, as well as its size and

67 HS August 14, 1982 Waterfront Agreement

scope, fluctuated wildly. The numbers bandied about ranged from 45 Million to $165 Million with every possible price variation in between.

By late summer 1980, The scope of the hotel and luxury conference center complex on the banks of the Hudson River near the foot of Main Street also fluctuated wildly, growing in magnitude to epic heights. In the local press, Wilbert Allen, the city's commissioner of development CDA went on record as being opposed to Yonkers Waterfront Associates.

The latest iteration of Yonkers of the Future took on the fantastic dimensions of an otherworldly Shangri La.

"The downtown waterfront complex would be practically a self-contained community with housing, shops, restaurants, a hotel and transportation, all within a five minute walk. The project would be built along the waterfront from the sugar house on the south to just past the Yonkers railroad stations on the north. The first building on the south would be 50 condominium townhouses, each containing three bedrooms, to be built over a 400-car parking garage. Next to this would be a riverfront hotel and club that would contain 375 rooms and be geared to the luxury and business market.

Farther north would be a conference center containing a 750-seat auditorium and meeting rooms capable of holding 600 more people. A 600-car parking garage would be built adjacent to the conference center. Across the railroad tracks from the conference center the former trolley car barn now used by the city as a garage would be transformed into a center for small shops, boutiques and food stalls. Just north of the conference center would be a combined tennis center, marine and retail center. A supermarket would be included among the shops.

West would be a renovated city pier, with the possibility of day liner and hydrofoil stops for connecting to Manhattan. There would also be a riverfront café and a separate restaurant. Rounding out the northern boundary of the project would be 500 units of one and two bedroom apartments approximately 24 stories high. The whole project would be built in phases, starting with the retail center, the conference center and a scaled-down hotel. Later the hotel would be expanded to its full 375 rooms and the housing, marina and other shops would be built. In all, the project would take five years to complete."[68]

Soon Wilbert Allen of the CDA would face his own problems when City Manager Sal Prezioso fired him. One reason cited was because of the lack of progress on the Waterfront project.[69] Allen

---

[68] HS Aug 28, 1980 Doubts remain as council nears waterfront vote
[69] HS Oct 11, 1982 The city's commissioner of development Wilbert Allen fired

had been moving too slowly in implementing the city and the CDA's role in the proposal put forth by Yonkers Waterfront Associates, but a stronger reason as to why Wilbert Allen may have been fired is because, he, like many others, was opposed to the exclusive contract in place with Yonkers Waterfront Associates. Wilbert Allen had made the mistake of accompanying Mayor Loehr to Miami on a fact-finding mission to look at projects that had been developed in part by Henry Silverman and Peter Edelman.[70]

All along Mayor Loehr had said the city should not link itself to Weintraub because of his legal problems in New York City.[71] As a result, in the next hearing of the Yonkers City Council, the Memorandum of Understanding with Yonkers Waterfront Associates was stalled. [72]

This time the heavy lifting came from union workers, where Weintraub's handiwork was evident. Arriving at a public hearing on the project that had been scheduled by the City Council, about 200 construction workers showed up. With the fervor of Trump supporters, armed with placards, chanting "We want jobs," they demanded speedy action and the removal of Mayor Loehr if none was taken. Peter Edelman responded that if the city approved the project it would mean at least

[70] HS July 29, 1980 Miami site to shed light on waterfront plan
[71] HS July 12, 1980 Loehr council caution on city waterfront plan
[72] HS August 4, 1980 Hearing Set on Waterfront Complex Project stalled no MOU

2,000 construction jobs.[73] The show of force appeared to be encouraged by union leaders throughout the country, although many of the group's leaders had conferred with the developers, and with Melvin Weintraub in particular.

Caving to union pressure, Mayor Loehr did a turnabout and supported the waterfront project. Addressing the construction workers, he said, "This is not a welfare project. This is a project that's good for you, good for us and good for the city." [74]

A few days later, The Yonkers City Council approved a $140 million hotel/conference center project for development on the city's waterfront. "The project hinged on the federal government to pick up the tab for half of the $39 million public share of the cost and the state governments waiving requirements for competitive bidding on construction contracts."[75] Within a seven-day time frame, the various numbers attributed to the project were $140 million, $155 Million, $160 million and $165 million.

By the time Yonkers Waterfront Associates ran into roadblocks related to money, the library had already been sent to its grave. Construction for the arterial was going as planned, but potential investors were not keen on a venture where the

---

[73] HS August 6, 1980 Angry Workers demand waterfront action
[74] HS Sept 3, 1980 Waterfront
[75] HS September 7, 1980 Waterfront Vote

immediate area surrounding the waterfront was inhabited by less than optimal dwellings. Buena Vista Avenue, in particular, was viewed as a slum and could theoretically be taken by eminent domain and bulldozed. Only there was a complication. Many people who lived in that area did not want to move, and City Council member Andrew MacDonald, representative of the 3rd ward, was skeptical of Melvin Weintraub and his sweetheart deal with the city to develop the waterfront.

All along Andrew MacDonald had been a thorn in Martinelli's side ever since he had proposed a resolution to save the library. Now the tension intensified every time Weintraub missed another deadline to come up with money to fund the project. MacDonald repeatedly called for an end to the city's deal with Weintraub. MacDonald was the only one to name the deal for what it was—the mayor's pet project which was "put forth in 1979 but remained perpetually in the planning stages,"[76] where it ultimately stalled. The project never left the planning phase for reasons that had little do to with Andrew MacDonald or the rundown buildings in his ward.

The project never left the planning phase because of Melvin Weintraub. When it comes to Weintraub, it's important to set the record straight.

[76] HS, Jan 1983 Campaign 83 is underway

Historically speaking and surprisingly, when Weintraub appeared on the scene in 1979 to ink the deal with the city, his company was somewhat heralded as a knight in shining armor, the arbiter of an exciting new vision for the city's neglected waterfront. History had indeed been kind to Mr. Weintraub.

In her book *Yonkers in the Twentieth Century*, Professor Marilyn E. Weigold, never identifies Melvin Weintraub as the developer for the waterfront project. It was noted that "S/E Asset Development, together with the Morelite Construction Company unveiled plans for a hotel, convention center, restaurants, a new recreation pier, restoration of the pier used by the Hudson River Day Line and refurbishing of the former trolley barn. Best of all, the developers were willing to put up a substantial amount of money for these projects."[77]

In reality, Weintraub didn't have any money, and due to his track record as a low-income real estate developer with a history of fraud, especially of defrauding government entities, no one wanted to give him any money. Like Donald Trump, Melvin Weintraub was a developer who had essentially bilked his investors. No one wanted to lend him any money, the same way investors shied

[77] **Weigold, Marilyn E., *Yonkers in the Twentieth Century* (Albany: SUNY Press, 2014), 177.**

away from Trump after the collapse of his investments in Atlantic City.

From 1974 to 1979 and again from 1982 to 1989, during Martinelli's reign as mayor, the city of Yonkers was perpetually on the brink of financial disaster. Even early in Martinelli's tenure as Mayor, an article in the New York Times criticized Martinelli for failing to deliver on his promise and asserted "Bank officials have asked the city why they should assist a municipality that faces default and yet refuses to raise its own taxes." [78]

Had Martinelli set forth an initiative to raise taxes, he would have alienated his base. Instead, he allowed the city to endure one fiscal crisis after another, rather than to risk losing his bid for reelection. Over the course of fifteen years, Yonkers was plagued by looming bankruptcy, and beset with wage freezes, repeated rounds of layoffs, and the revolving door practice of rehiring city personnel, the massive strikes waged by sanitation workers, teachers, librarians and fire fighters, and the forced closure of fire stations and library branches. While the city battled its never ending fiscal crisis, Martinelli forged ahead, spearheading his campaign to save the city by erecting a magnificent convention center and hotel complex on the waterfront. It was the equivalent

---

[78] **NYT, Nov 14, 1975 In Yonkers, a Question of Fiscal Leadership**

of playing the fiddle while this city of seven hills burned to the ground.

There were many things that went wrong with the waterfront project, but it really boiled down to both the city's and Weintraub's inability to raise money. The city was unable to do its part in the project by getting federal funding. A $20 million Urban Development Action Grant needed to be accompanied by "legally binding" private financing,[79]a Catch-22 because private financing was never going to happen. Weintraub made promises that private financing was imminent, but it never came through. At one point, it was thought development would begin if Weintraub came up with the letters that he said had been promised to him from two banks, Marine Midland and Barclay's. The promise of bank financing bought Yonkers Waterfront Associates (Weintraub) another extension, one among many and by no means the last time his exclusive contract with the city was kept in force. Soon Weintraub's deal with the city of Yonkers would be as dead as the library.

Even though it was clear that Martinelli's Yonkers of the Future wasn't going to happen with Yonkers Waterfront Associates, Weintraub was still wheeling and dealing with both Martinelli and the city on both the waterfront and on other

---

[79] **HS Feb 27, 1983 Still treading water**

projects. The same year that the library was destroyed, Melvin Weintraub—now acting through Morelite Construction Company instead of Yonkers Waterfront Associates—was given exclusive rights to develop the former site of School #4 even though other private companies offered more money. The 11-2 vote to sell the former school contradicted a policy set by the City Council in late 1981 (under Mayor Loehr) to sell property at a public auction whenever possible. Councilmen Michael F. Cipriani, R (9) and Nicholas V. Longo, R (12) co-sponsored a resolution that would permit the sale of School #4, without public bidding, to Morelite Construction (Weintraub's company) for $230,000. [80]

When the public hearing was held, a number of Yonkersites, most of whom were black, opposed the sale. These speakers described the racial segregation that existed in Yonkers, and how the sale to Weintraub continued the long-standing practice of systemic racism. The final speaker was white. He spoke of how blacks had ruined neighborhoods in the Bronx, claiming that the buildings originally were "in fine shape" but had "deteriorated" when the blacks moved in. The speaker then stated that he supported the sale to Weintraub because he didn't want the same thing to happen in Yonkers. In his closing remarks, he

---

[80] **United States vs. Yonkers Bd. of Educ. 624 F.Supp. 1276 (1985)**

stated, "I'm not a good speaker ... but I think you get the idea." The audience responded with an ovation. Martinelli supported Weintraub on the ground that people ought to "have a right ... to decide what happens to "their neighborhood.[81] This, however, had never been Martinelli's stance, with the community who tried to save the Carnegie Library.

Ultimately, the kibosh was put on Weintraub's project due the pending federal lawsuit brought by the Justice department against the city for racial discrimination in housing and education.

Surprisingly, the city limped along with Yonkers Waterfront Associates, giving Weintraub a vote of confidence even though bids for a federal grant needed to begin the project were twice rejected in 1981 and again in 1983 because Weintraub did not get private financing. What had begun as a 90-day exclusive designation for Weintraub has stretched for years. "The council approved extensions in 1979, 1980, 1981 and November 1982." [82]

During this time, Martinelli had his own legal problems. In the summer of 1982, The Securities and Exchange Commission went to court to try to force a securities magazine

---

[81] **Ibid.**

[82] **HS April 15, 1983 Strange Twist in confidence votes**

published by Martinelli to register as an investment adviser. The SEC filed a civil complaint in U.S. District Court in Washington D.C., alleging that *Stock Market Magazine*, published in Yonkers, had acted as an investment adviser to its readers but had failed to register as required by federal law. The magazine violated federal laws when it failed to disclose that the authors of some magazine articles were paid fees. In other words, the magazine was a "pay for play" in which P.R. people and freelance writers were paid to write favorable stories offering stock tips. Martinelli and his managing editor, Bernard Brown, countered the charges claiming they were "groundless and without substance." Martinelli called the charges "pure government harassment," essentially alleging they were trumped-up.[83]

Martinelli always had a good handle on the media. He knew how to deliver sound bites and possessed Teflon-coated armor; he knew how not to let anything negative stick to him. More importantly, through his own experience of being a mini media mogul, he knew how the media worked, or rather how to work it to his own benefit. Somehow the story of Martinelli's prosecution ended up on the United Press International (UPI wire) and came to the attention of James Kilpatrick, who wrote the nationally

---

[83] **HS, July 21, 1982, Martinelli Magazine taken to court by SEC**

syndicated column *A Conservative View* from Washington, D.C. Kirkpatrick came to Martinelli's defense, suggesting the SEC had no business regulating who could write about securities. Kilpatrick argued that the SEC was overstepping its bounds by regulating who was writing about stocks.[84] The real issue was disclosure—that Martinelli's articles were made up to look like real news without telling his readers the stories were concocted.

By 1985 the press continued to keep tabs on Weintraub who seemed to have his hands in everything connected to the waterfront. Suddenly the City Council was called to vote on major issues. Most of the discussion took place in the back room in a closed-door executive session. The Counsel of record, Arthur J. Doran, told council members the session was closed to the public because potential litigation was involved—that Weintraub would bring a lawsuit against the city if he didn't get what he wanted.

Then the Yonkers Industrial Development Agency agreed to sell up to $20 million in tax free bonds to fund the project. There was even talk again of developing a restaurant at City Pier. This is what prompted an emergency, barely legal, City Council meeting, done behind closed doors.

[84] **The Times News, Twin Falls, Idaho, August 7, 1984, Stocks Magazine Wrestles SEC Bear**

In secrecy, the Council voted 6-1 to give Weintraub a 99-year lease for exclusive use as a restaurant on the river's public recreation pier. The exclusive 99-year lease was granted to Weintraub even though work had stopped on the waterfront project due to lack of funding.[85] The grand vision for the Yonkers of the Future encompassing hotels, conference centers and luxury condominiums with day liner and hydrofoil transportation to Manhattan had been reduced to a restaurant. Even more surprising, the lease granted to Weintraub permanently closed the pier to free public access for ninety-nine years.

By December 1985, Weintraub was in trouble again. This time he was indicted in Florida on charges of bribery and conspiracy. The charges were related to his business dealings with Ronald Norman, former mayor of Sarasota, who had engaged in a consulting contract with Weintraub. The terms of the contract are murky. Weintraub claimed he made an initial payment of $2,000 and subsequent payments of $1,000 over two years while Norman helped guide a $25 million, multi-use business complex through the Sarasota Florida municipal process. The project remained incomplete. Weintraub told the press that he had been unfairly smeared as a result of the indictment. He also said, "he might reach a joint venture

---

[85] **HS April 21, 1985 Council Votes raise eyebrow**

agreement within a month that would get the Yonkers waterfront project moving forward after almost a year of inaction."[86]

In a later deal with the Mount Vernon Real estate company NCAS Realty Management Corp., Weintraub revealed his proposal to build a 2,000 unit condominium with Yonkers Waterfront Associates. The realty company never returned phone calls to talk to press and the Yonkers City Manager, Rodney Irwin, said, "It's not certain." Irwin did acknowledge that the City's Counsel, Arthur Doran, and Mayor Martinelli had met several times with NCAS Realty. The Realty company had proposed to immediately convert a former brick powerhouse into condominiums. The current plan for the gutted powerhouse to be developed as an office building with a small restaurant was scrapped. In the press, Doran said, "It was a business decision that condos would be better than an office building and had nothing to do with Weintraub's legal problems in Florida." According to an article in the Herald Statesman, when Weintraub was reached, he said, "I am working diligently to put together what is best for Yonkers, and whatever it is, it's going to be very good for Yonkers."[87]

---

[86] **HS December 15, 1985 Waterfront Developer says indictment is unfair**
[87] **HS Dec 31, 1985 Yonkers City Council approves of waterfront housing venture**

9
The Road to Nowhere

"They started the "bridge to nowhere" around (Greystone?) ...but never did anything about connecting it to the overpass. Our beautiful library was demolished for no reason..." - Ellen Cooke posted on Facebook I grew up in Yonkers, April 29, 2019

A one-man wrecking crew, anything Melvin Weintraub touched during his years of wheeling and dealing inevitably turned out to be not very good for Yonkers. Few projects proposed by Weintraub came to fruition. Now 92, Weintraub lives in Purchase, New York. When asked about the waterfront, he said, "We only did one building there." Then he added, "The Pierpointe was a rehab building. It was the first building on the entire river all the way up to Ossining." With a budget of $300 to $400 million Pierpointe was initially designed to attract investors. Getting the green light for the project proved problematic due to the pending federal litigation and fallout related to racial discrimination in housing and education. In 1988, in what appears to be a preemptive move on the part of Weintraub, Norwood Campbell became the first black partner of Yonkers Waterfront Associates. It was a common practice for white New York real estate developers to use a black person as a front, albeit a strategic partner, to get a project in compliance with civil rights and anti-discrimination regulations.

Pierpointe did get built amid public and civic protests that the complex would block views of the river from the center of the city. John Grosfeld, the architect of Pierpointe, said that vistas from the City Hall and from other central parts of the city would remain, said he had tried to shape the project "to benefit all of the community." [88] Pierpointe became an apartment complex available for rental; it is not a condominium offering units for sale. "The waterfront turned out beautiful," Weintraub opined. "It could have been earlier if it wasn't for Judge Sands (sic). He stopped the work being done there. [Building condominiums.] "That was a whole lifetime ago."

Weintraub blaming Judge Leonard Sand for his inability to get the waterfront project off the ground is ludicrous. Anything and everything that ever went wrong in Yonkers is blamed on Judge Sand. Whenever Sand's name is posted on the Facebook *I Grew Up in Yonkers* group page, the hateful comments posted against his name are the

---

[88] **NYT September 27, 1987, High Rise Draws Protests in Yonkers**

equivalent of Trump supporters chanting vitriol against immigrants, Muslims, liberals and democrats at a Trump rally. Leonard B. Sand is the federal judge in New York who presided over the landmark case that found Yonkers city officials had intentionally and systematically segregated public housing and schools along racial lines for nearly thirty years.[89]

In a completely different matter unrelated to development in Yonkers, in 1999 Weintraub got into legal trouble again and soon faced jail time. This time Weintraub was found guilty for violating the Clean Air Act by exploiting Mexican immigrants and other undocumented immigrants who were ordered to remove asbestos from a construction site. The workers were denied the protective garb required by safety regulations to save $117,000 on the asbestos removal. The workers "breathed large amounts of asbestos dust as they scraped, cut and clawed dry asbestos with crowbars and with their bare hands."[90]

Weintraub's companies Morelite Development and Liberty Realty were required to pay fines and Weintraub went to jail for a year. It was noted at sentencing that Weintraub showed no signs of remorse. [91]

---

[89] **NYT, Dec 5, 2016, Leonard B. Sand, Judge in Landmark Yonkers Segregation Case, Dies at 88.**
[90] **Hartford Courant May 12, 2000 Developer gets year in jail, fine**
[91] **Ibid.**

Today Weintraub takes full credit for the development of the Yonkers waterfront, but not for the many years of deception that blocked anything from getting done. He said, "I started the waterfront development. I started the whole thing down there. It took almost 15 years to get approved." There is no mention of the churning rehab projects, the recurring charges of fraud, or the lack of private investors that forestalled the project for years. His only explanation is "That was Yonkers. That was Yonkers," he said again, as if blaming Yonkers somehow exonerated him from any wrongdoing or responsibility.

The proposed development by Weintraub, his group the Yonkers Waterfront Associates and the city of Yonkers occurred during a time when the charges of influence peddling at the Department of Housing and Urban Development (HUD) were at an all-time-high, where instead of addressing the housing needs of America's poor, the flow of money from the federal government lined the coffers of slum landlords and real estate developers and the myriad of vendors who work for them, including but not limited to, consultants, architects, designers, engineers, unions and construction companies. Even during the Reagan years, when his administration tried to rein-in HUD spending, "Annual HUD outlays rose from $12.7 billion in 1980 to $18.5 billion in 1988."[92]

Many of these projects were already in the works before Reagan tried to put a lid on spending.

The sad thing about the long delay in the waterfront development is considering what could have been. The city missed opportunities with two highly credible developers who were interested in the Yonkers waterfront. Only Martinelli would not hear of it. The Radisson developers, including Jerome Garfield, Robert Schlageter (Network Enterprises Corp.), and the Radisson Hotel Group that at that time operated 19 hotels in the U.S., wanted to build a hotel and conference center on the waterfront. In 1979 the Radisson Group was rebuffed by then Mayor Angelo Martinelli. Later the Radisson Group was given a second opportunity by Mayor Loehr. In the past Loehr had not been able to get the City Council to back off on the commitment to Weintraub's group. In the meeting Loehr called with Radisson, only Andrew MacDonald was present, as representative of the 3rd ward, where the development was slated to take place. [93]Loehr was later accused by Weintraub of violating the agreement with Yonkers Waterfront Associates by entering discussions with the Radisson Group. [94]

---

[92] **Butler, Stuart M., Ph.D., The Heritage Foundation Abstract Reforming HUD to Prevent New Scandals July 27, 1989**

[93] **HS April 16, 1980 Loehr giving waterfront plan 2nd Chance**

[94] **HS April 22, 1980 PLANNERS**

MacDonald recalls that the Radisson developers were not the only viable contenders for the project. "There were planning (sessions) meetings with the Rouse Brothers." The Maryland-based Rouse Company had a proven track record with the Boston waterfront, the Baltimore waterfront, and thirty malls nationwide. According to MacDonald, "The Rouse Brothers developed the Baltimore waterfront and had the expertise and funding to develop the Yonkers waterfront but there was disagreement among City Council members. Rouse Brothers was not picked. A faction of the council wanted Mel Weintraub to exercise his five year exclusive right." At the time, Loehr requested that the Community Development Association (CDA) explain publicly why they had turned away the Rouse Company. Angelo Martinelli who, at that time sat on the board of the CDA, was unavailable for comment.[95]

Against all odds, the bromance between Martinelli and Weintraub blossomed. Even though Weintraub failed to deliver time and time again, Martinelli stuck with him. Martinelli badly wanted to realize his waterfront dream but would not allow anyone else but Weintraub to do the project. The question is why? When asked about his relationship with Martinelli, Weintraub said, "If it wasn't for Angelo Martinelli, nothing would have

[95] **HS October 7, 1979 Mayor Loehr Questions Developer Choice**

been built down there. He was a very good man! Ethical!" he emphasized. Andrew MacDonald recalled seeing Mel Weintraub with Angelo Martinelli in 2018 at a fundraising event for a city judge running for the New York State Supreme Court. "They were as tight as ever," MacDonald said.

Angelo Martinelli passed away in October 2018. He is credited with doing a lot of good for Yonkers, including funding the Untermyer Park Conservancy, and restoring the Temple of Love, formerly known as the Eagle's Nest, in memory of his wife Carol. Elected as Mayor six times, his image and likeness were featured in the HBO miniseries "Show Me a Hero," Lisa Belkin's account of the landmark case presided over by Judge Sand that thrust Yonkers and its young mayor Nicholas C. Wasicsko into a desegregation crisis. The story pulled no punches, depicting Yonkers in the late 1980s as a hotbed for racism.

Before Martinelli died, he could not be reached for comment about the Carnegie Library. Some people who spoke about his involvement with the library were reluctant to comment frankly until after his death. Several people interviewed said, "Don't quote me on this, but…." There was evidently fear of raising Martinelli's ire, the same way people walk on eggshells around Donald Trump.

When Weintraub was asked about the Carnegie Library, he said, "I have no knowledge of it. I don't know anything about the library." When Weintraub said he didn't know anything about the library, it's entirely possible that he is speaking the truth. The library meant nothing to him. And sadly, the library meant nothing to Angelo Martinelli.

Regarding the widening of Nepperhan Avenue, Weintraub said, "They had to do that. You can't go from east to west unless you use that road. And they did a lovely job," he added.

But they didn't do a lovely job. Andrew MacDonald describes the Nepperhan arterial as becoming the road to nowhere. "Instead of winding up north of the Sugar House and opening up access for the development of the waterfront, the road never got to Buena Vista. It became a four-lane road to nowhere." One more gaffe in a sequence of many.

Frank Cardone is explicit about the Nepperhan arterial as being the road to nowhere. "The newly aligned roadway was supposed to lead to the 'Superblock' (Prospect Street between Riverdale Avenue and Hawthorne Avenue). The belief was that the "Super Block" could reach its potential only with this alignment. Well, the library was demolished, and the "Superblock" remained vacant for many (20?) years."

Andrew MacDonald talked about what was intended versus what actually happened. "From Saw Mill all the traffic from the parkways would go down to the river and open up the waterfront for development. There were bits and pieces and fits and starts, but the major development never happened until after 2000."

Technically speaking, Prospect Street was supposed to play an important part in the development of the Yonkers waterfront. To the best of his recollection, Cardone said, "One plan called for a bridge that would take people over the railroad tracks to the waterfront. This bridge was never built and access to the now dramatically redeveloped waterfront is via the underpass at the foot of Main Street." Traveling to the waterfront via the Main Street underpass is the same as it has been for more than one hundred years. The library was demolished for nothing.

The irony is that the capitalist forces at work under Martinelli's leadership were largely inept. Had the irascible Andrew Carnegie witnessed the debacle, the demolition would have angered him. Carnegie would have respected the decision to destroy the library had it meant economic progress by reaping substantially larger financial rewards. In this instance, though, Carnegie would have been appalled at the bumbling incompetence of the public officials and the mess they made while trying to pander to their own self-interests.

10
Everyone in Yonkers is on the Take

"Make sure you mention BY NAME the sleazy, corrupt politicians who were responsible for the destruction of this unique and beautiful building." -Steve Zanzarella posted on Facebook I grew up in Yonkers, February 28, 2018

Returning to the cold day in April, when the Yonkers City Council agreed to hear Lee Hipius make her appeal to save the library, Frank Cardone was also there. When his turn came to speak, he remembers the council members as being polite. He also remembers Martinelli keeping his head down the entire time, until Cardone said, "Yonkers is the ugliest city. Aside from private homes and churches, Yonkers has very few outstanding buildings and the library is one of them." For a brief moment, Martinelli looked up and gave Cardone more than a passing glance.

During the discussion prior to voting, Martinelli characterized the issue as, in effect, "Building for the Future vs. Preserving the Past." The twelve-member Yonkers City Council was predominantly Republican (9 Republicans to 3

Democrats). In any initiative, Mayor Angelo Martinelli, a Republican, also got to vote along with the Council. Charles Cola, who had brought the resolution to save the library, along with Andrew Macdonald, was ill when the Council voted. The three voting on the side of the library were Andrew MacDonald (D), Peter Chema (R), and Bernice Spreckman (R). A vote of 9 to 3, with Martinelli, casting the 12th vote, sent the resolution to the Rules Committee, where it stayed, floundering until the library had been destroyed.

For the purpose of this article, a Public Disclosure Request (FOIA Request) was filed with the city of Yonkers to obtain records of the Yonkers City Council agenda and minutes for this time period. Deputy City Clerk Mike Ramondelli wrote "that a response providing an answer or denial, or a partial denial will be mailed within twenty business days." Five months later, no records and no further communication was provided by the city.

Other documents and testimony, though, do corroborate that this wasn't the first time that the Yonkers City Council of 1982 had a mashup along partisan lines. In the 1980s, the council members tended to vote not so much by their partisan affiliation and were instead more influenced by the demands of their constituency and their loyalty to Martinelli. While the formation of bipartisan coalitions is certainly healthy for democracy, it in no way altered the fate of the library, which had been condemned to death.

A Democrat, actually a Conservative Democrat, Andrew MacDonald described himself as "young and idealistic," like Don Quixote battling windmills. MacDonald represented the 3rd ward, close to the Getty Square area in the vicinity of Warburton Avenue, which ran parallel with the Hudson River.

MacDonald's ward lay smack in the end zone needed by the city to implement their grand plan for the Yonkers of the Future. In 1979, MacDonald easily won over the GOP candidate who had waged a write-in campaign that had opened when Councilman Gerry Loehr vacated to run for mayor and won. Loehr served the city as mayor from 1980-81 but had lost reelection to Martinelli.

One of the council members who voted to send the library resolution to the rules committee was Democrat Harry Oxman, who represented the 4th Ward, encompassing the Getty Square area, which was home to his small dry cleaning business that sat catty corner across the street from the Yonkers Carnegie Library. As the incumbent in the 1979 election, he easily defeated his Republican opponent. With his balding pate and chrome aviator eyeglasses, he was fond of wearing

Hawaiian shirts and ropey gold chain necklaces. Democrat Oxman tended to vote in alignment with Republican Mayor Martinelli. My Grandma Katherine lived in Oxman's ward, but I don't know if she had voted for him.

At the eleventh hour, a last ditch effort came to save the library, a reprieve that would have granted a stay of execution. Andrew MacDonald told me that New York State suddenly gave the city the option to seek another way to build the arterial and still preserve the library. "They could have rerouted and moved the street expansion farther south and not have taken the building," he said. The city could have taken Harry Oxman's dry cleaning business through eminent domain. Oxman opposed it vehemently and had the votes from most of the City Council members, and Martinelli's support.

Mayor Angelo Martinelli, Melvin Weintraub, and the City Council member Oxman, who owned a small-time dry cleaning business, formed an unlikely trio of strange bedfellows, all of whom had financial motives for wanting to see the library razed. Martinelli and Weintraub wanted to hasten the development of waterfront, and Oxman didn't want his business disrupted. So, they ran over the old library. But there was also money on the table that no one seemed to know about.

Tracking the facts revealed dirty dealings until the true pattern began to emerge. Weintraub had a stranglehold on the Yonkers waterfront, and the reasons were far darker than anyone could have imagined.

A *wiseguy* who asked to remain unnamed said, "Everyone in Yonkers was on the take."

Just days before the library went down, everyone knew it was too late to try to save it. Rhoda Breitbart, who was a librarian at the Carnegie Library, said, "When we talked to the mayor, he said it was too late to change the plan and they were running a state highway right through the building." My Grandma Katherine could not have known what was going on behind the scenes. I don't think anyone in Yonkers knew what was going on. Had people been aware of what was really taking place on the Yonkers waterfront, they would have been terrified.

Mary Hoar, President Emerita of the Yonkers Historical Society, recounts being the Mayor's Community Relations President from 1980-82. She remembers asking Martinelli if the library could be saved when it was days away from demolition. She had first been appointed President by Mayor Gerry Loehr. She stayed on after Angelo Martinelli was reelected, through to the end of 1982. At the time she was a member of the Yonkers Historical Society, but not a board member. "We didn't hear about the library coming down until a month prior to the actual demolition. At that point they had moved the library to the Genung's building. The Carnegie Library was no longer owned by Yonkers but owned by New York State. At the time, I learned they were taking down the library to widen the street, I saw the mayor a day or two later and said we had to do something to stop it from being taken down, but he said, 'It was just too late.'"

In the wake of the library's death, other interesting facts emerged. In 1987, the New York Times reported that the Justice department had indicted ten road-construction companies and ten of their executives on charges of conspiring to rig bids on road construction. Of the ten companies indicted, all of them were based in Westchester county. Nigro Brothers Inc. of Mount Vernon was among the ten.[96] It had been Nigro Construction that had been awarded the contract from New York State to demolish the library and reconstruct four-tenths-of-a-mile on the expansion of Nepperhan Avenue. At $3,942,268, Nigro was the low-bidder on the project that would begin around June,1982.[97] Adjusted for inflation, by today's valuation, Nigro's low-ball bid would be over $10 million.

---

[96] **NYT, June 26, 1987, U.S. Indicts ten companies on road bids**
[97] **NYT, April 4, 1982, Campaign to Save the Library**

The construction start date released to the press differed from what actually took place. According to eyewitnesses, the library's demolition was already underway in April. Andrew MacDonald mentioned that "Nigro Construction did a lot of work in Yonkers."

In the charges brought against Nigro Brothers and other construction companies, "Federal and state law-enforcement officials described the indictments as the most extensive involving bid-rigging by contractors in the state since the Justice Department started investigating road contracts in New York State in 1979."[98] Law enforcement officials stated the conspiracies involved contracts totaling more than $100 million.[99] A mong the city, the state and Nigro Construction, the money that had changed hands made it impossible to turn back the clock on the library. Martinelli was right when he said, "It was just too late."

It was too late for my Grandma Katherine too. A fire burned her tenement to the ground. It was arson. Fortunately, she wasn't there at the time. She had moved into low-income, public housing close to Schlobohm, which was one of the first projects to be built in Yonkers. Her tenement couldn't be sold. Banks didn't give loans to buyers

---

[98] **NYT, June 26, 1987, U.S. Indicts ten companies on road bids**
[99] **Ibid.**

for homes in neighborhoods that had been redlined. We later found she had saved $90,000 and stashed it under her steps. As a survivor of the Great Depression, she didn't trust banks.

Money launderers also do not trust banks. My task of following the money grew more bizarre when I learned of Weintraub's stranglehold on the waterfront. In a startling revelation, a 2018 news story in Lohud claimed that the Yonkers waterfront was formally investigated in the 1980s for being rife with organized crime. Court documents revealed that former Genovese crime boss Vincent "The Chin" Gigante was forced to intervene in a feud between two crime-family factions to take control of the city's then-undeveloped Hudson River waterfront.

Reportedly, Gigante solved a dispute between two warring mafia families, the Genovese and Lucchese, by ordering a payment of $400,00 made to Daniel Pagano of the Genovese family to surrender his claim on waterfront property. "Federal investigators said wiretaps and confidential informants suggested that Lucchese capo Steven Crea Sr. ultimately wrested control of the property from none other than Melvin Weintraub.[100]

There is alarming concern, but equally pathetic and comic elements, that can be associated

---

[100] **HS August 4, 1980 Hearing Set on Waterfront Complex Project stalled no MOU**

with the sudden apparition of "The Chin" Gigante wearing his bathrobe and slippers, padding around the Yonkers waterfront, making peace among the warring tribes. Other members from both the Genovese and Lucchese families were linked to bribes involving a construction project in northeast Yonkers. Urban myth or fact? One thing is certain—Gigante maintained enormous influence in the Bronx, Yonkers and upper Westchester. In Yonkers it was common knowledge that the garbage and construction industries were controlled by organized crime. In 1980 when 200 construction workers turned out in an organized protest to the stalled waterfront project in order to intimidate Mayor Gerry Loehr, there need not be speculation as to how they got there.

Whether the boys from the 'hood (*those who know them who know*) were using strong arm tactics to maintain control over the waterfront cannot be proven. "The Chin" and others connected to him were not big on writing memos, holding press conferences, or using phones that could be subject to wiretapping. One thing, though, is certain, after the demolition of the library, the Nepperhan arterial led to nowhere and the development on the waterfront was stalled for years.

11
Was the Library its Own Worst Enemy?

"I spent a lot of time there and felt violated when it was torn down. More than a terrible waste, it was a criminal act against the community." – Ralph DiCarpio posted in Facebook I grew up in Yonkers, May 5, 2018

Was the Yonkers Public Library responsible for its own demise? There aren't many people around now who have actually worked at the Carnegie library. Although many years have passed, some oral testimonies can be cobbled together, describing how the people who had held the library close to their hearts experienced the death of their library.

Grinton I. Will was much more than an ordinary librarian or the former director of the Yonkers Public Library; tall, trim, with well-coiffed hair parted on the side and a spare moustache, he was well known and respected among the library community on a global scale, a Librarian's librarian. Erudite, clever and very much a gentleman,

Grinton Will was savvy enough about relationship-building to get the $2.5 million funding from the city of Yonkers to build the Sprain Brook (Grassy Sprain) Branch that first opened in 1962. This library branch has since been renamed the Grinton I. Will branch in his honor.

For years, Will had also tried to convince the city to fund a new main branch library downtown to replace the Carnegie building. Since the days of the perennial librarian Miss Helen Blodget, the Carnegie library had been declared to be too small. Though just because a library is small, it's not sufficient reason to put it to death. Will might have wanted to see a larger, modern facility in downtown Yonkers, but that did not mean he wanted to see the Carnegie Library stomped to the ground. In an archived interview Will said, "he had written about it in the Herald Statesman many times, but no one was paying any attention."

Although a fraction of Carnegie libraries has been razed, today many of these buildings are still standing and continue to operate as libraries. Some library buildings, have been converted to museums, civic offices, schools, and churches. There is even one college dormitory in Schenectady, New York and a Church Youth Center in Decatur, Alabama.

Eugene Howell, who is currently a librarian with the Yonkers Public Library, recounted how when he and his family first moved to Downtown Yonkers as a child in 1964, Grinton Will's office in the Carnegie Library was located directly across the street. Eugene's parents could see into the children's room from their bedroom, so they were never worried about where he was if he stayed out late. Howell said, "Grinton Will was curious to know who the Negro boy was (at that time we were called 'colored'), always reading the local history collection in front of his office. After I introduced myself, our friendship took off."

Eugene Howell was nine years old when he first met Mr. Will. Over the years, Will recognized something of a kindred spirit in Howell, and became a mentor to him. Before Grinton Will retired, he had asked Eugene Howell to come "into the service" at the library, but Howell said he was too afraid to join because he thought he wouldn't measure up to his standards. "Well, I was wrong," he admits, "And he was right," Howell chuckled. He ended up staying with the Yonkers Public library for forty-three years and rose up through the ranks. "I've been in the library in all of its manifestations I think he would be proud of my service." In fact, Howell said laughing, "I'm sure of it!"

In his oral transcript, Grinton Will remembers trying to get people together to go to Albany to speak out to get the building made into a historical landmark. The timing of Will's visit to Albany might have had something to do with why at the last minute the state offered Yonkers' public officials the option of rerouting the arterial. But that would have meant taking Council member Oxman's dry cleaners by eminent domain, and that was never going to be a possibility so long as Oxman had Martinelli's protection. According to Will, only fourteen people appeared at the hearing about the library. The New York State Department of Transportation (NYSDOT) showed up and said, "It seemed like nobody cares, so what."

People did care about losing the library, but their interest was loose and rambling, often fragmented; it's not that they couldn't take the prospect of losing the library seriously, they didn't know what to do. They didn't know how to form a coalition as strong and as ruthless as their opponents that would have saved the library from death. The Yonkersites who wanted to save the library are similar to all of the disparate factions in America who feel duty bound to save our democracy from tyranny.

In the final summation of why the library was razed, Andrew MacDonald noted, "It was done for an economic proposition and took down a beautiful building that did not have to come down."

Historical accounts don't reflect what really happened with the library. Marilyn E. Weigold, who wrote *Yonkers in the Twentieth Century,* said, "While the loss was a terrible blow to many people in Yonkers it was in the whole scheme of urban development, it may not have been viewed as a one of the most significant though one of the most unfortunate developments. The larger goal was to redevelop the city."

Redevelop the city indeed. Michael Rebic has a different perspective, "The reality back then was there was this really big problem in the city of Yonkers. The planning bureau would study the situation and advise the city what they should do and the right way to do it." Rebic remembers politicians who interfered constantly, telling him and others that their jobs were on the line. "They would all come in and tell us what we were going to do and interfered constantly. Preserving the library did not coalesce with the interests of eastern Yonkers that had become the dominant political power."

There is collective cultural embarrassment that the library was taken away from the Yonkers community. In Joan Jennings' and Luis Perelman's book *Images of Yonkers*, it was noted in a photo caption that featured the library, "The library was demolished in 1982 to accommodate the widening of the Nepperhan Avenue arterial. That demolition is generally considered to be one of Yonkers's most shameful moments."[101]

Marilyn Weigold's book *Yonkers in the Twentieth Century* was commissioned by the Yonkers Historical Society and numerous patrons and supporters, including Angelo Martinelli. In the book, there is hardly mention of the Carnegie library. Weigold explained, "The Library was not a significant part of my research. Since the manuscript was read by historical society board members, had they recommended that I include more information about the library I would have done so."

Although Rebic had been hired to preserve buildings like the Carnegie library, he was put into a very difficult position. "I don't think Michael Rebic could have done more than he did to save the library," Lee Hipius said. "Not with Martinelli around. If he had, he would have lost his job." When dealing with the library, Rebic was essentially obstructed from doing his job. He remembers one day when he was working, Lee Hipius had brought him some cupcakes she had made. He was afraid to accept them because he never knew who would be watching. "And, I was getting some blow-back on my campaign to save the library, which was my job," he said.

---

[101] **Jennings, Joan; Perelman, Luis, Images of Yonkers, (Charleston, South Carolina: Arcadia Publishing, 2013) 49.**

Rebic had been invited to attend a fundraiser, but his boss Phil Pistone warned him to stay away. Pistone told Rebic, "Michael, be careful, you might be dealing with things you don't know about." No one really discussed politics, Rebic notes, but in Yonkers politics was very important. Rebic viewed the political machinery and its base of supporters as being all about destruction and destroying. He found it hard to accept that downtown Yonkers was not seen for what it was—"a very vital place." It just wasn't what middle class white people from east Yonkers wanted. The new social class on the east side was afraid to go to downtown Yonkers. The entire initiative was about social class and a power base in east Yonkers. There was no concern about the viability of the community of Southwest Yonkers and preserving the vitality of its downtown.

Angelo Martinelli and Robert Moses shared something in common. Their decisions failed to take into account the needs of the community and exhibited reckless disregard for the common good. Instead, their decisions were made largely to benefit their own self-interest. What the Carnegie Library meant to Martinelli was the same as what the Brooklyn Dodgers meant to Robert Moses. Nothing. Martinelli's idea of the true beacon of the city was the Yonkers Raceway. In Weigold's book, Martinelli talks about the Yonkers Raceway as being a "beacon," and "a light on the Thruway." "It really represents what Yonkers is all about," he said. [102] He sounds like a goodfella who wants to bet on the horses because he likes the action. Moving books down the street to the old Genung's building made money for everyone. By knocking down the library and building a road to nowhere, everyone got a piece of the action.

Martinelli didn't get the idea that this beautiful historic library was the city's true beacon, any more than Moses understood why baseball, America's favorite pastime, was important to so many people. Too bad Jane Jacobs wasn't around to save Ebbets Field. When Robert Moses wanted to build the multilane "Broome Street Expressway" to connect New Jersey through the Holland tunnel to the Manhattan and Williamsburg Bridges, his plan required the expansion of Fifth Avenue, similar to the expansion of Nepperhan Avenue to create an arterial. Instead of slicing through the heart of the library, Moses' plan cut into Washington Square Park in the center of Greenwich Village. This plan was eligible for 90% federal funding, not unlike the expansion of the Yonkers Nepperhan Avenue arterial that was funded by New York State to turn the library into rubble.

[102] Weigold, Marilyn E., *Yonkers in the Twentieth Century* (Albany: SUNY Press, 2014), 336.

Teardowns, demolitions and expansions are favored by politicians, construction companies, labor unions and real estate developers because everyone makes money, although it's not transparent just how much money is made. The cronyism, on the other hand, that played out between Angelo Martinelli and Melvin Weintraub, can be easily deduced from the pattern of incontrovertible evidence showing facts that speak for themselves.

Jane Jacobs, with her silver bobbed haircut and heavy black framed coke-bottle glasses, was another variation of Lee Hipius. Both were activists, women of intelligence and compassion with a strong moral compass. The difference between Jane Jacobs and Lee Hipius's work with the Committee to Save the Library: Ms. Jacobs was able to form a sophisticated coalition among the community that included local politicos, the powerful residents who lived in Greenwich Village, academics, pundits, and the press. Jacobs' battle against Robert Moses and his Broome Street Expressway lasted nine years and is said to be have been the primary stress factor that ultimately led to his death.

12
Big and powerful enough to fight City Hall

"You may blame the politicians, but the people also should have stepped forward and stopped it." - Larry Moore posted on Facebook I grew up in Yonkers Oct 12, 2018

The death of the Yonkers Carnegie Library is a cautionary tale of what happens when people who are fighting for what is right are unable to form a solid, unstoppable coalition that will defeat the bad guys. There has to be a common vision, a common goal, and a common message that is never distracted by tangential or lesser subordinate issues. If the mission is to save the library, then save the library. If our current fight is to save democracy, then save our democracy. The tyranny of Donald Trump and the stranglehold of the GOP must be defeated before we can address the most important issues of our times, including, but not limited to, climate change, health care, the jobs of the future, and our fundamental civil liberties. As Jane Jacobs once said, "A district has to be big and powerful enough to fight city hall." [103]

Today in the era of Trump, we show signs of what Jane Jacobs defined as "rushing headlong into a Dark Age."[104] Some pundits have made a strong argument suggesting that Jane Jacobs' book *Dark Age Ahead*, may have predicted the rise of Trump. One current indicator is the mass amnesia shown by the alt right factions of our culture and the GOP who no longer remember the core principles of our democracy. Another worrisome indicator is what Jacobs defined as the 'cultural xenophobia' or the fear and loathing of minorities that occurs when a society is in decline. This was evidenced by the horrific racism exhibited in Yonkers in the era of Martinelli as much as it exists today in the era of Trump against Muslims, Mexicans and any people of color regardless of their national origins.

Was the demolition of the library due to racism? The long-term practice and pattern of discrimination in public housing caused the value of the library to be diminished and degraded in the eyes of the white power brokers. The razing of the library was not due to a single racist act, but it was the logical outcome of long-term, systemic racism. The real fault of the library wasn't that it was in the

---

103 Jacobs, Jane, The Death and Life of Great American Cities, (New York: Random House, 1961).
104 Jacobs Jane, Dark Age Ahead, (New York: Random House, 2004)

wrong place—blocking the proposed Nepperhan Avenue arterial; it was located in the wrong neighborhood, one that had been largely concentrated with people who were brown or black and had been purposefully segregated from the city's power base on the east side.

Reiterating the sentiment of the Carnegie Library's founding father, John Brennan, the library welcomed all "All races, the rich and the poor." In 1904 the library was founded in good faith as a face of democracy, offering the proposition that all men were created equal. In a sense, John Brennan echoed the same principles of liberty as espoused by Abraham Lincoln in the Gettysburg address: "Fourscore and seven years ago our fathers brought forth, on this continent, a new nation, conceived in liberty, and dedicated to the proposition that all men are created equal."

Abraham Lincoln used the term "proposition" because he knew that the proposition that all men are created equal is something Americans have to fight for again and again.[105] We can't ever take the proposition of equality for granted, not for the nation, a state, a city, or a small town. Americans always have to be on guard that they are safeguarding their liberty, even if it is only to save a library.

Rhoda Breitbart, who was a librarian at the

[105] **Wilson, Douglas L., Lincoln's Sword, (New York: Random House, 2006).**

Carnegie Library said, "One of the most heartbreaking moments was watching that old Carnegie Library come down. It broke my heart and it shouldn't have happened." After the library was destroyed, many people felt like they had been punched in the stomach and had the wind knocked out. It was similar to the way so many people felt when Trump was elected as President. In both instances, democracy had been dealt a deadly blow. For well over a hundred years, Yonkers, has always had a rich diversity of people, with wide-ranging incomes and backgrounds. Regardless of color or ethnicity, the working-class and poor of Yonkers have always been imbued with a civic pride for being smart, streetwise and hardworking. Yet among people who have not had the experience of dealing with egregiously self-interested power brokers, there is the pervasive feeling that you can't fight city hall, that you can't win.

Do the bad guys always win? Most of the time, they do. But by building the right coalition armed with the right knowledge, and by fighting with the fervor of winning a game (or a war) for the gipper, good guys can win too. Everyone can take a lesson from Jane Jacobs. When pitted against the ultimate power broker, Robert Moses, she won.

Many years have passed, but people who had held the library close to their hearts have never really gotten over its death. All of the people who could have come together to stop the demolition were, for one reason or another, unable to form a cohesive movement to save the library. The Yonkersites who wanted to save the library are similar to the disparate factions in America today who want to save our democracy from tyranny, but so far have been unable to form a focused coalition.

Other people tried to save the library. Some could not be reached for comment. Others like Henry J. Mazzeo Jr. have since passed away. Mazzeo, a copywriter and author, had been mentioned in the New York Times as being an enthusiastic member of the Committee to Save the Public Library. Lee Hipius, Frank Cardone, Michael Rebic, Andrew MacDonald, and others put up a heroic fight. By pounding the pavement, standing in front of grocery stores, railroad stations, and bus stops, they gathered over 5,000 signatures to save the building. What they lacked was the ability to connect with the many different power bases and fragmented factions in Yonkers to coalesce and build a united front. Even if they had formed a powerful coalition, it is not certain whether their battle could have turned around the sequence of missteps—one gaffe after another—that led to the library's catastrophic failure.

Rebic acknowledges that the lesson learned

in the loss of the library later resulted in saving Phillipse Manor. The state was going to defund Phillipse Manor and close it. Built in 1682, Phillipse Manor is the oldest building in Westchester county. Today it is a historic museum that still stands in downtown Yonkers. Rebic realized in the fight to save Phillipse Manor that it was not enough to mobilize the west of Yonkers but that influencers from all over the city, and especially the east side of Yonkers, had to be mobilized as well. When the committee was able to get people from the east side to join the fight, a solid coalition saved the building and Phillipse Manor was preserved.

Some remnants of the Carnegie library are still floating around. After the demolition, the three lunettes painted by David C. Hutchison that had been hung from the upper walls of the children's room went into storage at the Hudson River Museum. One mural is on display at the Grinton I. Will branch of the Yonkers Public Library. Other building remnants include the three cartouche wreaths that are on public display in Washington Park, up the hill between the War Memorial Monument and City Hall on South Broadway. The library once had a fourth wreath, but there is speculation it was destroyed during the demolition. The whereabouts of some elements of the building, specifically the terracotta, granite, and the marble, are unknown, but presumably Nigro Construction had a plan for salvage and garbage disposal; these two industries were joined at the hip under the watchful eye of Vincent "The Chin" Gigante.

The Getty Square of today bears no resemblance to the downtown Yonkers of yesteryear. The old tenements, quaint storefronts, and public buildings are gone. St. Mary's Church (The Church of the Immaculate Conception), where the Rev Charley once railed against the vicissitudes of Andrew Carnegie, now holds Catholic mass in Spanish and serves a sizable Hispanic population mainly from Puerto Rico and the Dominican Republic.

The Getty Square area of downtown Yonkers, including the waterfront, bears no resemblance to Martinelli's vison for Yonkers of the Future. There is no conference center, luxury high-rise condominiums, upscale hotels and restaurants, or a gambling casino. There is no day liner and hydrofoil commute connecting to Manhattan. Instead cookie cutter, high-rise, relatively high-end apartment buildings, line the banks of the Hudson River like a wall. Dramatically different from the 1980s, the Yonkers waterfront is ideally situated for a mobile community—people who want to be within an easy commute to Manhattan and pay rent month-to-month. A portion of the Saw Mill River has been daylighted and courses like a steady stream through Getty Square. The Riverfront Branch of the Yonkers Public Library was built on the site of the old Otis Elevator factory building, opening to the public in 2002.

Eugene Howell, who was mentored by Grinton Will, was on the long range planning committee for the Riverfront Library. Howell attributes his role in building the new library as a tribute to the visionary ability of Mr. Will. He said, "He knew what would sustain the library and let it grow." He added that Mr. Will recognized something "transformative in me." It is only fitting that Mr. Howell, whose entire life revolved around the library, should find himself in the position of playing a large role in building the Riverfront library.

The design of the Riverfront library is contemporary, and while it is beautiful and much larger than the old Carnegie Library, old-timers miss the original building. Soon in another decade, no one will remember the Carnegie Library. Nor will they remember the old tenements, brownstones, and other historic buildings like Loew's Theater that used to inhabit Southwest Yonkers. Even though no one will remember, history still matters. So long as democracy is a viable proposition worth fighting for, what happened to the library will always matter.

Sidat Balgobin, whose mother Pearl worked at the library, spoke softly about the long-lasting impact the library had made on his life. He went to Lehigh University and later went to Yale Divinity School where he fell in love with the old Missions Library because it reminded him of the Yonkers Carnegie Library. "The beauty of the Yonkers Carnegie Library got into my bones and into my psyche," he said. After he started his ministry, he moved to Norwich, Connecticut. One day he got a call from the Otis Library asking him to be on their board. Soon it became apparent that the library was in "poor condition" and in need of "renovation." So, he headed up the committee to raise money for the renovation. He knew it was the right thing to do. There were plans in place with a budget of $3 million. The actual renovation cost over $10 million. Today the Otis Library is more than a library and has become a thriving cultural center. "All of this, [my involvement with the Otis Library] was motivated from my memory of the Yonkers Carnegie Library."

Sidat Balgobin passed away in 2018, but his gentle, wise words linger behind. "The true loss of the Yonkers Library is when we lose a piece of history and beauty, it affects generations to come. They robbed children of a birthright. They robbed them of an environment that inspired them to become better [people]. That was the true loss. It was not about losing bricks and mortars; the library was something that feeds us well into adulthood."

My Grandma Katherine is long dead now. Seeing the library knocked flat to the ground hurt her. As the years went on, I don't think she could turn away from that hole in the ground. I think the site of where the library once stood is where her heart is buried.

Today Lee Hipius is still in the same book discussion group that started years ago at the Carnegie Library. Her book club meets once a month. Only this past year, they took off the month of July off because of the heat. She loves to read. "I do love to read, hear and see a lot of things that people might miss if they didn't read." She thinks today, so many people have their faces stuck in their devices, "little magic wizards," that they don't see what's going on around them. She worries about our democracy. She believes in life, liberty and the pursuit of happiness. She believes in the U.S. Constitution and the Bill of Rights. "We have to remind ourselves of what's important, otherwise we'll lose what we have," she said.

The loss of the library still affects her. She remembers that day in April so long ago when she saw where one side of the library had been bashed in, the death knell of what was yet to come. She walks along the footprint of where the library once stood. Each year, when the time comes to pay her taxes, she always goes to the Yonkers City Hall to pay in person. By approaching city hall from behind the building, she does not have to try cross the street in time to make the light. On the way, she walks along the footprint of where the library used to be. "It's all gone now, and I always feel sad." To this day, she still envisions the upstairs and downstairs, but it's gone. "It's like Michael Rebic used to say, 'Once it's gone, it's gone.'"

From T.S. Elliot The Waste Land

I. The Burial of the Dead

April is the cruelest month, breeding
Lilacs out of the dead land, mixing
Memory and desire, stirring
Dull roots with spring rain.
Winter kept us warm, covering
Earth in forgetful snow, feeding
A little life with dried tubers.

Bibliography

Books

Anderson, Martin, The Federal Bulldozer: A Critical Analysis of Urban Renewal, 1942-1962 (MIT Press 1964).

Bobinski, George S., Carnegie Libraries: Their History and Impact on American Public Library Development, (Chicago: American Library Association, 1969).

Caro, Robert A., The Power Broker: Robert Moses and the Fall of New York, (New York: Vintage Books, 1975).

Eliot, T.S., The Waste Land, (London: The Criterion,1922)

Hartman, Chester. Squires, Gregory D., *The Integration Debate Competing Futures for American Cities*, (New York: Routledge, 2010).

Jacobs, Jane, The Death and Life of Great American Cities, (New York: Random House, 1961).

Jacobs Jane, Dark Age Ahead, (New York: Random House, 2004).

Jennings, Joan; Perelman, Luis, Images of Yonkers, (Charleston, South Carolina: Arcadia Publishing, 2013).

Koch, Theodore Wesley, A Book of Carnegie Libraries (New York: The H.W Wilson Company, 1917).

Jones, Theodore, Carnegie Libraries Across American: A Public Legacy, (New York: John Wiley & Sons, Inc., 1997).

Queenan, Joe. One For The Books, (New York: Viking 2012).

Rebic, Michael P., Landmarks Lost & Found: An Introduction to the Architecture and History of Yonkers, (Yonkers, NY: Yonkers Planning Bureau, 1986).

Rothstein, Richard. *The Color of Law*, (New York: Liveright Publishing, 2017).

Tucker, PhD, Phillip Thomas, *Pickett's Charge: A new look at Gettysburg's final attack*, (New York: Skyhorse Publishing, 2016), 361.

Yonkers Historical Society and the Blue Door Artist Association, *Yonkers Then & Now*, (Charleston, South Carolina: Arcadia Publishing, 2008).

Van Slyck, Abigail A., Free to All: Carnegie Libraries & American Culture 1890 – 1920 (Chicago: University of Chicago Press, 1995).

Weigold, Marilyn E., and the Yonkers Historical Society, *Yonkers in the Twentieth Century*, (Albany, New York: SUNY Press 2014).

Wilson, Douglas L., *Lincoln's Sword*, (New York: Random House, 2006).

News Articles:

Yonkers Statesman, March 12, 1901, Public Library Building Assured.

The Yonkers Statesman, Friday, May 3, 1901, Carnegie Library Sites.

The Yonkers Statesman, June 20, 1903, Carnegie Library.

Yonkers Statesman, January 23, 1929, Library Report Again Decries Lack of Room.

The Atlantic, January 1945, Slums and City Planning by Robert Moses.

Herald Statesman (hereinafter HS) Westchester Commerce & Industry, January 19, 1965.

HS, April 26, 1966, Community Renewal Program Offers Hope for Downtown.

New York Times (hereinafter NYT), Jan 19, 1972, Indicted by City in Loan Scandals.

NYT, Nov 14, 1975 In Yonkers, a Question of Fiscal Leadership.

HS May 25 1979 Developers eye site on waterfront—given exclusive rights!!!

HS August 13, 1979 Firebombing!

HS August 9, 1979, 3 eliminated as suspects in fire which drove out family.

HS August 17, 1979 politicians again assailed in arson death aftermath.

HS, Sept 12, 1979 $45 million proposal unveiled for waterfront.

HS October 7, 1979 Mayor Loehr Questions Developer Choice.

HS Oct 17, 1979 Waterfront Public Hearing.

HS OCT 28, 1979 Library Relocation Project in Full Swing by staff writer Jim Cavanaugh, Library Relocation Project in Full Swing.

HS Dec 4, 1979 CDA Inquiry.

HS Jan 21, 1980 Waterfront Questions.

HS April 16 1980 Loehr giving waterfront plan 2nd Chance.

HS April 22, 1980 PLANNERS.

HS, Sept 23, 1980, Developers ink agreement on proposed waterfront center.

HS Oct 26, 1980 Shoddy work Mars Library Renovations.

NYT April 17, 1981, Commentary on Yonkers.

NYT, April 17, 1981, Harassed Mayor Rolls with the Punches.

NYT, July 30, 1981, Robert Moses, Master Builder, is Dead at 92.

HS Nov 16, 1981 Angelo R. Martinelli Mayor-elect talks candidly about himself.

HS, Nov 17, 1981, Loehr Proposes Scrapping Waterfront Proposal.

NYT April 4, 1982 Campaign to Save Yonkers Library, Ian T. Macauley.

HS August 14, 1982 Waterfront Agreement.

HS, Jan 1983 Campaign 83 is underway.

HS Feb 27, 1983 Still treading water.

HS March 3, 1983 School Sale.

HS April 15 ,1983 Strange Twist in confidence votes.

HS, July 21, 1982, Martinelli Magazine taken to court by SEC.

The Times News, Twin Falls, Idaho, August 7, 1984, Stocks Magazine Wrestles SEC Bear.

NYT Nov 21, 1985, Judge Finds Yonkers Has a Segregation Policy.

NYT, June 29, 1986, Developers are Rediscovering Yonkers.

NYT, June 26, 1987, U.S. Indicts ten companies on road bids.

NYT September 27, 1987, High Rise Draws Protests in Yonkers.

NYT, Dec 22, 1987, Yonkers in Anguish: Black and White in 2 Worlds.

Washington Post Aug 8, 1988, Judge Holds Yonkers in Contempt.

NYT, Aug 11, 1988, As Blacks in Yonkers See it—Time to Say You're Wrong.

NYT Oct 7, 1989 Conscience and Law in Yonkers.

NYT, May 19, 1990, The H.U.D Scandal: Widening?

NYT, July 22, 1990, The Region: H.U.D. scandal's Lesson: It's a Long Road from Revelation to Resolution.

NYT, May 20, 2007, In Yonkers We Trust.
PBS, Jan 17, 2013, The Legacy of Robert Moses.

Lohud, Sept 8, 2015, Yonkers Civil Rights Activist Winston Ross dies.

NYT, Dec 5, 2016, Leonard B. Sand, Judge in Landmark Yonkers Segregation Case, Dies at 88.

City Lab, Dec 20, 2016, Did Jane Jacobs Predict the Rise of Trump?

Gothamist, June 2, 2017, Why Robert Moses is to Blame for Losing the Brooklyn Dodgers to L.A.

Lohud, March 28, 2018, Mobbed up: Lower Hudson Valley's Historical Ties to Las Cosa Nostra.

Websites

The Secret History of Scarsdale, August 13, 2014, Joshua Cockburn The Final Voyage as Captain of the Yarmouth and the fall of Marcus Garvey. https://thomas-quirk.com/2014/08/13/joshua-cockburn-the-final-voyage-as-captain-of-the-yarmouth-and-the-fall-of-marcus-garvey/

Legal Citations

UNITED STATES v. YONKERS BD. OF EDUC., 624 F.Supp. 1276 (1985).

Yonkers 1996; US. V. City of Yonkers 96 F.3d 600, (2d Cir. 1996).

Abstracts

Butler, Stuart M., Ph.D., The Heritage Foundation Abstract Reforming HUD to Prevent New Scandals July 27, 1989.

Favareau, John, Notes re: History of Yonkers Public Library

U.S. Census Data, NYS, Westchester County, Yonkers, 1960

U.S. Census Data, NYS, Westchester County, Yonkers, 1980

Periodicals

Flynn, Tom, Yonkers Historical Society Newsletter, Volume 2, Issue 3 Fall 1993, *Yonkers Public Library Centennial.*

Flynn, Rosalie, Yonkers Historical Society Newsletter, Summer 1996, *Carnegie Library Lunettes.*

Rebic, Michael P., The Westchester Historian, Quarterly of the Westchester County Historical Society, Volume 62, Fall 1986, Number 4, Yonkers and the Public Bath Movement.

Rebic, Michael P., The Westchester Historian, Quarterly of the Westchester County Historical Society, Volume 68, Number 3, Summer 1992, Living Conditions for Yonkers' Working Class in 1896.

Trinity Times, The Newsletter of the Presbyterian Church, May 2012, *David Chapel Hutchinson.*

Photos

Yonkers Carnegie Library from Wikimedia Commons, the free media repository.

Interviews

Sidat Balgobin, Sept 20, 2016.

Frank Cardone, Nov 28, 2016, Dec 4, 2016, May 28, 2019, June 3, 2019.

Tony Clark, July 8, 2019.

John Favareau, May 20, 2019, June 3, 2019, June 10, 2019, June 18, 2019, June 25, 2019.

Elizabeth Lee Hipius, Sept 6, 2016, June 5, 2019, July 18, 2019.

Mary Hoar, President Emerita of the Yonkers Historical Society, July 24, 2019.

Eugene Howell, July 11, 2019.

Andrew MacDonald, May 20, 2019.

Michael P. Rebic, Sept 20, 2016, June 1, 2019, July 18, 2019.

Marilyn E. Weigold, July 5, 2019.

Melvin Weintraub, July 3, 2019, July 5, 2019.

Jeffrey Williams, Oct 9, 2016, Oct 11, 2016.

Grinton I. Will and his wife Clarissa L. Will talk about the demolition of the Yonkers Carnegie Library.

Yonkers Public Library, "Interview about the Demolition of the Carnegie Library," YONKERS PUBLIC LIBRARY ARCHIVE, accessed May 13, 2019, http://archive.ypl.org/items/show/558.

Grinton I. Will talks about his career as a director of the Yonkers Public Library.
Yonkers Public Library, "Interview with Grinton I. Will about being a director of the Yonkers Public Library," YONKERS PUBLIC LIBRARY ARCHIVE, accessed May 13, 2019, http://archive.ypl.org/items/show/559.

Social Media
Facebook Community page *I grew up in Yonkers, New York!*
https://www.facebook.com/groups/IGUIyonkers/

INDEX

A

C

D

E

F

G

H

I

J

L

M

N

O

P

R

S

T

U

Y

Made in the USA
Coppell, TX
06 January 2021

47672579R20111